BRYAN ROBERTS & HEATHER KOLB

# DIGITAL NATIVES

## RAISING AN ONLINE GENERATION

# DIGITAL NATIVES
*Raising an Online Generation*
© Copyright by Pure Desire Ministries

Printed in the United States of America
ALL RIGHTS RESERVED
www.puredesire.org

**Published by**
Pure Desire Ministries International
www.puredesire.org | Gresham, Oregon | January 2018

ISBN 978-1-943291-03-8

# | CONTENTS

# WE SHOULD HAVE TAKEN THE BLUE PILL

Have you ever gone to see a movie and had no idea what it was about? I don't mean that you didn't know the ending or a clever plot twist; I mean no clue—no idea. It's a pretty rare occurrence nowadays given the amount of hype and publicity the movie industry pours into a production, not to mention the countless forms of mainstream and social media reviews (#spoileralert). It has only happened to me a handful of times and it's usually with a predictable chick flick that my wife wants to see.

There was however this one time: my dad and I had an afternoon to kill and we decided to see what was playing at the local theater. We walked up to the box office and began perusing the titles. I can't remember any of the movies playing. Nothing really jumped out at me. Dad said, "What about the one starting in 10 minutes?" I looked at the movie he was pointing to on the billboard: "*The Matrix*, hmm…I wonder what that's about?" "Sure, why not," I said unsuspectingly. I can honestly tell you that, not only do I feel privileged, but I'm quite proud of the fact that watching *The Matrix* for the first time was a completely unexpected adventure. I still remember my amazement while watching the opening scene. It was a bit dark, but otherwise nothing seemed out of sorts. That is until Trinity, unarmed and surrounded by five cops with guns, jumped into the air; time froze, the camera did this crazy 360 move and in two seconds, everyone, but Trinity, was laying on the ground KO-ed.

For the next 90 minutes I didn't move. I was mesmerized with never before seen computer generated graphics and crazy green screen camera tricks. But most captivating was the presentation of the plot. It wasn't a new plot—mostly a twist on another favorite movie of mine, *The Terminator*.[1] What blew my mind was how well the director communicated the innocuous nature of the computers, a stark contrast from *The Terminator*. *The Terminator* was an in-your-face, Arnold Schwarzenegger—"I'll be back"— the world is going to end, nothing is stopping that robot, we're all going to die and there is no hope, terrifying kind of movie.

*The Matrix* had just as much, if not more, dystopian despair, but no one knew it. All of the copper-tops were busily going about their routine, completely unaware of the reality surrounding them. No one but Neo, and his rebel freedom-fighter friends, understood the symbiotic tension between the machines and the humans. The machines produced a believable reality for the humans to feel content. Life was worth living and not questioning. In return, the humans fed the machines power to function. Both man and machine were literally on each other's life-support system. My favorite quote from *The Matrix* is, "I wish I had taken the blue pill."[2] In other words, I wish I could go back the blissful world of ignorance.

I'm writing this book because I believe I have been privy to a unique perspective about the Internet: how most of us use it

---

[1] Cameron, J. (1984). *The Terminator*. Hemdale Film Corporation.

[2] Wachowski, L. & Wachowski, L. (1999). *The Matrix*. Silver Pictures.

and how it uses us. My goal is to impart my observations and encourage every reader to have your own Neo-esk awakening. I want to empower Internet users to make informed choices when using this amazing tool of connection and technology. It's worth noting that I'm not a doomsday-conspiracist, prophesying the end of the world via the evil Internet. I don't believe the Internet is inherently evil; however, I've noticed that it tends to mirror the most impulsive version of our society.

I think the average Internet user has little if any idea how the Internet works. Furthermore, I believe that most parents, school counselors, social workers, and youth pastors (to name a few) are ill-equipped to teach kids about healthy responsible Internet use. Today, the Internet is probably one of the toughest challenges faced by parents and anyone who works closely with the teen population. As a parent of a grade schooler and a teenager, I recognize that those in the current generation are digital natives; they do not understand a world without the influence of the Internet, while their parents grew up in a world with little, if any, online influence. My kids view the altered reality the machines give us as normal.

For the last seven years, I have had the privilege of serving at a faith-based nonprofit organization, whose primary function is to help a struggling church get a handle on the monster of pornography. I have encountered countless individuals—men and women, young and old—who are living off of the machines altered reality. Some know that something is off but just can't quite figure it out, while others are living in hell and want out. But no matter how hard they try, they can't unplug.

I have not always worked in ministry or nonprofit. Prior to working at Pure Desire I was a laser engineer working for the aerospace industry. Computers were my life. My unusual background has given me a rare glimpse into not only the workings of the Internet, but also how church culture is uniquely prone to be ensnared in destructive online behavior. You might say that I feel like Neo: awakened to a daunting view of the powerful machines created by us to literally suck the life out of us. Meanwhile, most people I connect with have no idea they are trapped. If I am honest about what I know to be true, there are times I wish had taken the blue pill and didn't know the ugly truth about the Internet:[3,4,5]

- 65 percent of graduating high school seniors have engaged in sexual intercourse.

- 50 percent of all college students report having engaged in oral sex one or more times in the past 30 days.

- 93 percent of boys and 62 percent of girls are exposed to Internet pornography before the age of 18.

- 69 percent of boys and 55 percent of girls have seen pornography showing same-sex intercourse.

- 32 percent of boys and 18 percent of girls have viewed bestiality on the Internet.

- 15 percent of boys and 9 percent of girls have seen child pornography.

- Only 3 percent of college freshman who are males and 17 percent of females have never seen Internet pornography.

---

[3] Centers for Disease Control and Prevention (2013). "Youth Risk Behavior Survey." U.S. Department of Health and Human Services.

[4] Hoffman, K., Berntson, M. & Luff, T. (2014). "The Impact of Peers and Perceptions on Hooking Up." *College Student Affairs Journal, 32*(1), 129-140.

[5] Sabina, C., Wolak, J. & Finkelhor, D. (2008). "The Nature and Dynamics of Internet Pornography Exposure for Youth." *CyberPsychology and Behavior, 11*(6), 691-693.

- 39 percent of all teens and 59 percent of young adults have sent or posted sexually suggestive messages or pictures online.

The statistics are overwhelming and terrifying. You may even find yourself disputing or dismissing the numbers. Perhaps you would say, "Not my kids; not in my home; not in my school; not in my church." Let me assure you that the numbers are real. I have lost count of the times a pastor, a church leader, or a parent or a spouse have connected with Pure Desire after discovering that someone they are close to has a double life of pornography, or a sexual relationship outside of marriage, connected via the Internet.

We are past the point of asking, "Is there a problem?" The question we need to ask is, "What will we choose to do about the problem of Internet pornography?" Specifically, how do we as parents and grandparents, school counselors and teachers, and leaders in the church positively influence the next generation? It's a simple question to ask; however, the answer is anything but simple.

This book was written for the sole purpose of answering the question of how we can positively influence the next generation. I do realize that at this very moment you might be saying to yourself, "Positively influence the next generation? That's not why I picked up this book. I just want to know how to protect my kids from porn! Where's the off switch, or how do I pull the plug? Can't we just lock this sucker down! What if I just restrict my kids from using the computer?"

The unfortunate truth is that the Internet is not something to lock up, unplug, or shut down. The Internet is more than a browser on your desktop. It is not restricted to a set of applications. The Internet is not just a series of networks spanning the globe, or common data protocol. It's not a social platform or mass of searchable data. The Internet can best be summed up as the modern fruition of a reality: Anything. Anytime. Anywhere.

It is a powerful reality and one that our modern society is pursuing at an astonishing pace. Again, the Internet is not inherently evil. Without "Anything, Anytime, Anywhere," we would still be using paper maps and asking gas station attendants for directions, paying ridiculous long distance phone and cable TV bills, and using postcards and letters to communicate with family and friends.

Thanks to "Anything, Anytime, Anywhere" our news, media and entertainment are delivered instantly. Financial transactions are simplified, cost less, and are updated in real time. All levels of education, from grade school to graduate school, are accessible to the world at little or no cost other than the connection. Even the process of purchasing goods and services has become more cost and time effective. And, these are only a few of the most obvious ways the Internet has positively changed our world.

When parents say, "How do I protect my child from the Internet?" they are asking the wrong question. It's almost like saying, "How can I make sure my child is never involved in a car accident?" I know that seems like a ridiculous comparison, but it's actually quite accurate.

The average American will be in a car accident about once every 18 years, and automobile accidents are the fourth leading cause of death in the United States.[6] So how does this work? Most likely, you are not surprised by these two auto safety statistics, but at the same time, there is a high probability that there are two of these death machines (cars) sitting in your driveway.[7]

---

[6] Centers for Disease Control and Prevention. "Leading Cause of Death 2015." Retrieved from http://www.cdc.gov/nchs/fastats/leading-causes-of-death.htm

[7] IAC Publishing, LLC. (2017). "How many cars does the average American family own?" Retrieved from https://www.reference.com/world-view/many-cars-average-american-family-own-f0e6dffd882f2857

Why do the vast majority of Americans drive cars if, as a result, they are likely to be harmed by them several times throughout the course their life? The simple answer is that the automobiles, just like the Internet, are a fundamental necessity of our modern lives—so much so that most families could not imagine their daily lives without their cars. For the vast majority of Americans, most of the things we do—getting to work; driving the kids to soccer, ballet, and church; going shopping; enjoying weekend getaways; visiting friends and family; getting to the doctor; seeing a movie; and a hundred other things—would not be possible without our cars.

There are many interesting parallels between the automobile and the digital age. Both have radically modernized our world. Both historically separate generational norms. In the 1930s, you could have probably published a book called *Automobile Natives: Raising a Generation That Does Not Understand the World Without Cars.*

In the early 1900s, much of the world was not ready for the automobile, nor did they understand the great potential of efficient transportation. One of Henry Ford's most famous quotes is, "If I had asked people what they wanted, they would have said faster horses." As Ford developed the Model A and seven subsequent models before releasing the Model T, somewhere along the line Americans realized the car wasn't simply a faster horse. The automobile, more than any other invention of the nineteenth century, embodied the concept of "Anything, Anytime, Anywhere" in the twentieth century. In the same way, the invention of the Internet in the twentieth century is radically redefining the concept of "Anything, Anytime, Anywhere" in the twenty-first century.

Now, you might be asking yourself, "What about seat belts, air bags, and crumple zones?" These are all safety features designed to keep the driver and passenger safe in the event of an accident. If we are going to draw a parallel between the automobile era and digital era, why not compare these auto safety features to content filters and accountability software? The truth is that this is a great comparison, but it is important to note that these auto safety features are not designed to avoid accidents or compensate for reckless behavior.

To continue the analogy, the only way to effectively reduce accidents in the first place is driver education. Seatbelts or airbags have little, if any, positive effect when you drive your car off a 1,000-foot cliff at 100 miles per hour. Likewise, a seatbelt is also only effective when used. A recent study of driver education programs compared young drivers that had completed driver's education with those who had not.[8] The study found that young drivers who have not completed driver's education are:

- 75 percent more likely to get a traffic ticket.

- 24 percent more likely to be involved in a fatal or injury accident.

- 16 percent more likely to cause an accident.

The reason I cite these statistics is the point of the analogy: content filters and accountability apps (or safety features) are useless without the knowledge and motivation to use them. In Deuteronomy 6:7 (AMP), Moses gives the Israelites great insight for imparting knowledge to the next generation:

---

[8] Reed, L. (2015). Study: "Driver's ed significantly reduces teen crashes, tickets." University of Nebraska-Lincoln. Retrieved from http://newsroom.unl.edu/releases/2015/08/13/Study:+Driver's+ed+significantly+reduces+teen+crashes,+tickets

*You shall teach them diligently to your children [impressing God's precepts on their minds and penetrating their hearts with His truths] and shall speak of them when you sit in your house and when you walk on the road and when you lie down and when you get up.*

This text is a continuation of Moses' charge to Israel to serve their God faithfully. There are two very important elements to note in this passage: First, this charge was to the adult population, not children. This message is especially important to fathers whom God calls to be the head of the house. If we are going to teach our children healthy Internet use, we must lead by example. Parents, especially fathers, need to model appropriate Internet use, as well as the application of safety features (filters and accountability software).

Secondly, Moses does not say, "Lock up all your gold and valuables so that when your kids get tired of worshiping the one true God, they don't run off to make a golden calf and start worshiping it." He does just the opposite. He says, "Hey, we all know God's top Ten Commandments, so don't spend all your efforts preaching at your kids. The goal is to make God's Commandments more than knowledge—"impressing God's precepts on their minds." He takes it up a notch and says, "and penetrating their hearts." Meaning you've got to make training your kids a heart issue as well.

This is, essentially, driver's education. It is our job as parents, school administrators, teachers, and leaders to train our youth while they are "behind the wheel." It is useless to have a long list of rules and restrictions and say, "Okay, everything is safe and locked down; there's no way for you to get in trouble now." It would be like telling kids today, "Here is a really safe go-cart that you can only drive on an isolated track by yourself," and then thinking, *Okay, check driver's education off the list!* This solution would be great as long as those kids never grow up and need to drive a real car on the open road. In this book, we are going to cover both safety measures, good rules and practices, as well as a driver's education of sorts—how to drive defensively, guarding your heart.

The book is divided into four sections:

- **The nature of the Internet:** How did the Internet come into being, and how does it work?

- **The effect of the Internet:** We are going to look at some key studies and statistics that help explain the effect the Internet has had on our world socially, economically, and neurologically.

- **Practical solutions:** Given what we know about how the Internet works and its effects on our world, how can positive influence occur?

- **What's next:** What is the next development phase of the Internet and how can we best prepare to use it in a healthy way?

If the purpose of this book is to help us *positively influence the next generation*, then understanding the Internet is not enough. We have to understand what the Internet is doing to our kids, and those we impact, at a physiological level; we have to raise an awareness of the neurological changes that are happening in the brain as a result of the Internet. For this reason, I have asked Heather Kolb to join me in this venture, imparting her knowledge and area of expertise on the neurological, psychological, and behavioral aspects of Internet use.

My prayer for you, and for the youth you influence, is that God would use this resource to enlighten and encourage you. May the investment you make in the next generation spark a change in our world to seek knowledge and truth, producing a greater understanding of God in a deeper dimension.

Bryan Roberts

# A BRIEF HISTORY
# OF THE INTERNET

### YOU CAN ONLY KNOW WHERE YOU'RE GOING
### IF YOU KNOW WHERE YOU'VE BEEN.
#### JAMES BURKE[9]

It's pretty astonishing if you stop and think about how fast the Internet is growing. There are so many things that each of us rely on as part of everyday life that simply would not exist if not for the Internet. Many of these things didn't even exist 10 years ago: Smartphones (iPhones, Android devices), social media (Facebook, Twitter, Instagram), YouTube, Google Maps, eReaders (Kindle, iBooks, Google Books), and Cloud storage (Google Drive, Dropbox, iCloud) just to name a few.

If you look back 20 years, the digital landscape would be almost unrecognizable compared to today's standards. Just two decades ago, cameras used film that had to be taken out of the camera and dropped off at the local developer. You would then have to wait a week and pay a lot of money to get your pictures,

---

[9]  Burke, J. (1978). *Connections*. New York, NY: Simon & Schuster Paperbacks.

at least half of which you would throw out due to blur, red eyes, or a real nice shot of your thumb. It's so funny to think that now, when my family goes to Disneyland, we all have smart devices. We snap hundreds of photos, delete the ones we don't like, and instantly post a few on Facebook, where, within a matter of minutes, my mom will comment on how much she loves her grandkids and she can't believe how fast they're growing up. All the while, this entire photo sharing experience costs nothing.

Living in Portland, most of our trips to "The Happiest Place on Earth" are usually a 15-hour road trip I like to call "The Most Stress-Filled Drive on Earth," hauling two kids, two dogs and an RV. I don't know how my parents did it, but 30 years ago they used a paper map (no GPS), and put up with 15 hours of my sister and me comparing how many times we could ask, "Are we there yet?" or yelling at the other one, "STOP TOUCHING ME!" When my wife and I took the trip last year, I had my favorite Google Music playlist blaring through the speakers connected to the car via bluetooth. Meanwhile, Google Maps was tracking my location, periodically turning my music down so the nice navigation lady could let me know to expect a turn or traffic ahead. I don't think my kids ever once asked, "Are we there yet?" They were much too interested in watching their favorite movie or playing their favorite game on their tablets. My wife thoroughly enjoyed listening to her classical Spotify station (much more sophisticated than my music) while reading a book on her tablet.

Twenty years ago, movies were on VHS tapes that you could pretty much watch only at home on your enormous VHS player. When you were done watching the movie, you had to always "be kind and rewind" or people at the video store would be very unhappy with you. If you needed to call someone, you got out the phone book or Rolodex. I used to know the phone numbers of all of my friends. I think the only number I can remember now belongs to my parents, who have had the same number for more than 30 years connected to a landline. Actually, I switched them over to a digital line about five years ago, but don't tell them (Baby Boomers love their landlines).

Remember when you would pass notes to your friends during school? That ended with text messaging. My daughter says the kids at youth group are not allowed to use cell phones because everyone is constantly texting each other. This summer, my wife took my 10-year-old son and his two cousins to a museum. In one of the hallways between exhibits the boys ran into a pay phone. They were completely perplexed; one asked, "What is this thing?" while the other thought it was part of an exhibit. When my wife told them it was a public pay phone, they couldn't figure it out. They questioned, "Why you would pay to call someone?" and "Why wouldn't you just use your cell phone?"

Given the vast number of technological advances, you could easily write an entire multi-volume book series entitled *Stuff We Didn't Have 20 Years Ago*. My purpose in communicating these anecdotal examples is to make the point to every adult reading this book: if your kids or the kids you influence were born after the year 2000—Generation Z—they are digital natives. What is a digital native? Simply put: a person who does not know the world without the influence of the Internet. Generation Z can be identified by three main characteristics:

- They do not understand a world without the Internet.
- They do not know how to gain information without the Internet.
- They do not know how to relate with other people outside of the Internet.

Looking at the history of the Internet there are several important events that make the Internet what it is today. As much as I would love to nerd out in this chapter and explore the origins of the Internet in great detail, my editor explicitly stated that if I write about open architecture networking, transmission control protocol, or packet switching, the red pen would come out. So I'm going to keep it basic. For the purpose of this book, I want to touch on some of the major historical events that make the Internet what it is today and the effect it has on its users, especially kids. On the off chance that you want to know a comprehensive history of the Internet, there are a number of great articles published by the Internet Society: www.internetsociety.org.

## THE INTERNET IS BORN

The Internet was started by the United States (U.S.) Department of Defense.[10] So technically, if your kid's online behavior is concerning you, feel free to call your congressional representative to file a formal complaint—no guarantees on the effectiveness of that approach to positively affect your kid's online behavior. In the 1960s, the U.S. government started awarding contracts to universities and laboratories to develop ARPANET (Advanced Research Projects Agency Network). The goal of this project was to get computers in different locations to talk to each other via a universal network. The first message sent over the ARPANET was from a computer at the University of California, Los Angeles, to another computer at Stanford Research Institute. It may seem strange to think that getting computers to talk to each other is

---

[10] Andrews, E. (2013). "Who invented the internet?" Ask History. Retrieved from http://www.history.com/news/ask-history/who-invented-the-internet

that big a deal. Today, we don't think twice about accessing the same information on our smartphone that we get off our laptop. However, in the 1960s, this was a totally foreign concept.

Computers were built by a number of different manufacturers who each had different software, hardware, and approaches to communication driven by the application for which the computer was designed. Also, at that time, the phone companies owned all of the communication networks and essentially were still working off a point-to-point network—the switchboard operator model. This is where each device, which at the time was a telephone, would be connected directly from one caller to another.

Even as phone companies replaced switchboard operators with machines and computers, the network essentially operated in the same way: connecting one caller to another through a central hub. In the first 30 years of the Internet, developing it into the structure we know today, the approach of point-to-point networking and application-specific computers, was replaced by a universal network, where each device has access to every other device and all devices are compatible. These two elements are foundational to the Internet and set the stage for the next major evolution of the Internet: technological convergence.

Technological convergence, or more commonly referred to as convergence[11] is the concept that every device is connected to the Internet and will uniquely communicate information to the user. Today, you can access the same Internet from your TV, laptop, tablet, phone, watch, game console, and many other devices. Even newer cars and home automation systems access the Internet. All of these devices connect to the Internet and

---

[11] Author Unknown (2017). "Technological Convergence." Retrieved from https://en.wikipedia.org/wiki/Technological_convergence.

return information to the user: your phone will remind you about the calendar event scheduled on your laptop.

On your way to the meeting, your car can look up directions and traffic patterns to get you to the event on time. Your watch will upload data about how many steps it took to get from the parking lot to the event meeting location. Your tablet will provide a convenient way to see the meeting agenda and take notes without having to take out the bulky laptop.

On your way home, your phone can tell your house to turn on the heat, and when you arrive, it can tell your house to unlock the front door. After a long day, you can unwind with your online friends and your favorite role-playing game on your game console. Although this scenario may sound like an episode from *The Jetsons*, all of this technology is readily available and all driven by the Internet.

## 1.2 ZETTABYTES?

Even though the concept of convergence was fundamental to the structure of the Internet from the beginning, the fruition of universal networking and compatibility took a relatively long time to develop.[12] The idea and proof of concept was in place, but until the early 2000s, storage space, processing speed, and Internet connectivity were very expensive compared to today's standards. As these costs began to drop, the Internet exploded with information. As of 1993, there was barely over half an exabyte (half a billion gigabytes) of data accessible on the Internet. Ten years later, in 2003, there was eight times the

---

[12] Greenhaw, A. (2010). "How Big Is the Internet?" https://andygreenhaw.wordpress.com/tag/how-much-data-exists-online/.

amount of data (nearly five exabytes) on the Internet. Over the next four years, into 2007, the Internet grew steadily to nineteen exabytes. Around 2007 things took off. In just nine years, the Internet grew by a factor of 70 times to a total of 1.2 zettabytes (1.3 trillion gigabytes).

This number is a bit mind-boggling to think about. One way to understand it would be to take an iPad and fill all of the memory on that iPad. Then, set that iPad on the ground. Grab another iPad and fill it full and stack it on the first iPad. If you were to keep filling and stacking iPads until the data stored on those iPads equaled 1.2 zettabytes, the stack of iPads would be 339 miles high stretching well into the exosphere; about 110 miles above the orbit of the International Space Station.[13]

Anything you want to know is on the Internet. Information has become so abundant, and quickly accessible, that almost overnight the word "Google" went from being a noun to a verb. This information revolution happened so dramatically that the current generation has no concept of the value of information. Generation Z has more access to information than any previous generation. This is why they are conditioned to gather all of their information from the Internet.

## PLUG ME IN! _

By the end of 1969, ARPANET had four universities hosting a connection via telephone lines.[14] Over the next 10 years, the

---

[13] Greenhaw, A. (2010). "How Big Is the Internet?" https://andygreenhaw.wordpress.com/tag/how-much-data-exists-online/

[14] Zimmermann, K. & Emspak, J. (2017). "Internet History Timeline: ARPANET to the World Wide Web." Retrieved from https://www.livescience.com/20727-internet-history.html

number of host connections grew steadily to about 200. As the number of hosts grew and began to share information, more universities and businesses wanted access to a connection. The problem was that phone lines were not only slow, but because of the monopoly of phone companies operated by Bell Systems, they were extremely expensive.

In 1982, Bell Systems was deregulated, allowing phone companies to offer more competitive pricing for data lines on their network, allowing the Internet to grow at a much faster pace. Over the next 20 years, communications companies started to gain interest to investing new infrastructure for the fledgling Internet. By the year 2004, the Internet had more than one billion connections. Since 2004, the number of Internet connections has grown steadily, reaching 3.5 billion users—nearly half of the world's population.[15] To put that number in perspective, 100 years after Ford's Model T entered the market, only 1 billion people owned a car.

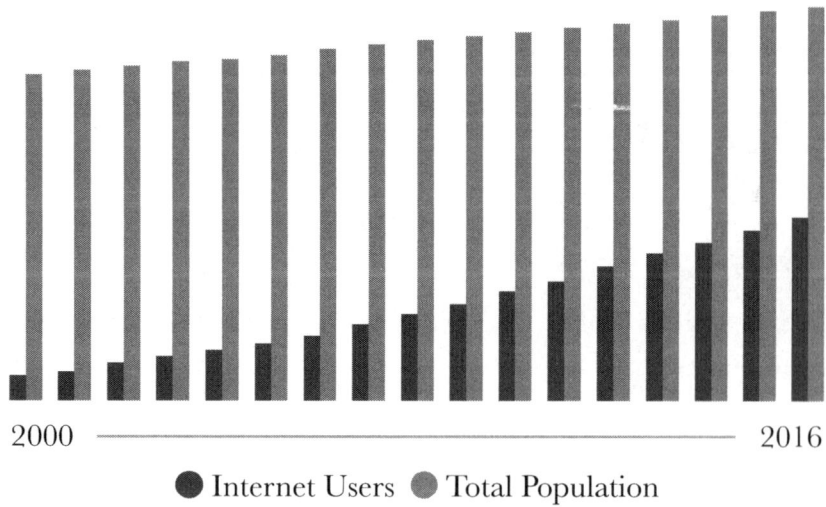

2000 ———————————————————————————— 2016

● Internet Users  ● Total Population

---

[15] Internet World Stats. (2017, December 4). *Internet Growth Statistics.* Retrieved from http://www.internetworldstats.com/emarketing.htm

Internet companies are so committed to connecting every human on the planet, they will go to extreme measures in the most remote parts of the world. In 2013, Google started the Loon Project.[16] Loon uses high-altitude balloons placed in the stratosphere to create an aerial wireless network. This is just one example of many that underline the powerful motivation Internet companies have to connect every human in the world.

## THE INTERNET MARKETPLACE

Although the most basic version of the Internet we currently experience (known as the World Wide Web) has existed for more than 25 years, the prevalence and development of the Internet as we know it has only existed for the last 15 years. More than half of the most popular websites and applications did not exist 15 years ago: Facebook, Twitter, YouTube, Wikipedia, Reddit, Pinterest, and Instagram, just to name a few. In the last 10 years, especially, there has been a dramatic shift in how Internet companies approach the market. For example, Netflix, founded in 1997, had a business model designed to compete with Blockbuster and Hollywood Video, shipping DVDs to customers. In 2007, they offered streaming video. In just nine years, DVD shipments dropped to less than 10 percent of their business operations. Google, the largest search service in the last 12 years, has launched a staggering number of services, which, for the most part, are entirely free to Internet users.

---

[16] "Project Loon." (2017, July 21). In Wikipedia, the Free Encyclopedia. Retrieved from https://en.wikipedia.org/wiki/Project_Loon

| | | | |
|---|---|---|---|
| 2004 | Google Gmail | 2011 | Google Music |
| 2005 | Google Maps | 2011 | Google Plus |
| 2006 | Google Calendar | 2012 | Google Now |
| 2007 | Google Docs | 2012 | Google Drive |
| 2008 | Google Chrome | 2013 | Google Hangouts |
| 2009 | Google Voice | 2015 | Google Photos |

In my professional opinion, the shift that Netflix and Google have made in their offerings and business model was a direct response to the dot-com bubble. Starting in 1997 until 2000, venture capitalist saw the Internet's steady growth and began to invest heavily into just about any start-up Internet company, no matter how ridiculous the business plan (assuming there was a business plan). The idea was that the Internet was a totally new market ripe for the picking. Investors really had no experience reading the market.

One online bookstore site saw its stock price soar by more than 1,000 percent in one week simply by announcing an updated website.[17] Eventually, when users realized that the vast majority of dot-com era companies didn't offer anything significantly different than brick and mortar stores, the market began to falter and over-investment led to a collapse of the market. The Internet companies that survived that dot-com bubble (Google, Netflix, eBay, Amazon), as well as newcomers to the market (Facebook, Twitter, YouTube, Reddit) saw that the Internet marketplace wasn't just a virtual version of a store that already existed. The market is not about retail: it's about advertising. The power of the Internet is information. All of the successful Internet companies of the last decade understand this concept well.

---

[17] Kennard, F. & Hanne, A. (2015). *Boom & Bust: A Look at Economic Bubbles*. Lulu.com.

Google understands it better than anyone: 95 percent of Google's income comes from advertising revenue.[18] Their effectiveness in advertising comes from knowing their users. The better they know their users, the more effective their advertising will be. In 2004, Google started personalized search. When a user requests a Google search, the returned results are custom-tailored to the user and their interest. How does Google know the user's interest? The answer is their amazing suite of free apps. Let's use me as an example: When I—along with about 1 billion other users—use Gmail as my email provider, Google gets to read my mail. When I schedule events, Google Calendar knows my daily routine. Google Music, Books, and Movies tells Google the kind of music I like, the books I read, and the movies I watch. Google Maps knows where I live, where I work, and anywhere else I go with a cell phone. Google Search knows what I'm looking for on the Internet. Google Plus knows who I'm friends with. Google Fit knows what I eat, how I exercise, and how healthy (or not healthy) I am.

Now, you might be saying, "That's it! No Google apps! No Google accounts for me!" Unfortunately, that's much easier said than done. After the dot-com bust and the success of targeted marketing, Internet companies like Google began to not only acquire a ton of money but also a ton of great talent. This combination of the best talent and nearly unlimited development budgets started a dramatic shift in the software industry, which super-charged Google's targeted marketing. In an amazingly short period of time, Google moved from most popular search engine

---

[18] Rudolph, S. (2014). "How Effective Is Online Advertising (Infographic)?" Business 2 Community. Retrieved from http://www.business2community.com/infographics/effective-online-advertising- 0996804#FMjdheFmTl3Ri7XZ.97.

to most popular web experience. With the launch of the Chrome browser in 2008 and Chromebook computers in 2011, Google has drastically altered how we use the Internet. The most glaring evidence is to look at browser usage statistics over the last 10 years.[19]

In 2007, Internet Explorer by Microsoft (IE) had virtually no competition. Today, IE is barely a blip on the radar of browser stats falling into the category of other browsers you've never heard of like Opera, Camino, SeaMonkey, etc. It's important to note that today Microsoft Windows is still the most widely used operating system, currently owning nearly 80 percent market share.[20] That means that four out of every five computers currently sold are preloaded with IE (or Microsoft Edge, the latest version of IE) as their default browser, and yet 95 percent of users who purchase those computers will go out of their way to use a different browser. Google is extremely good at knowing what Internet users want. In less than 10 years they have made IE into the most popular browser used to download Google Chrome.

 **BROWSER USAGE**

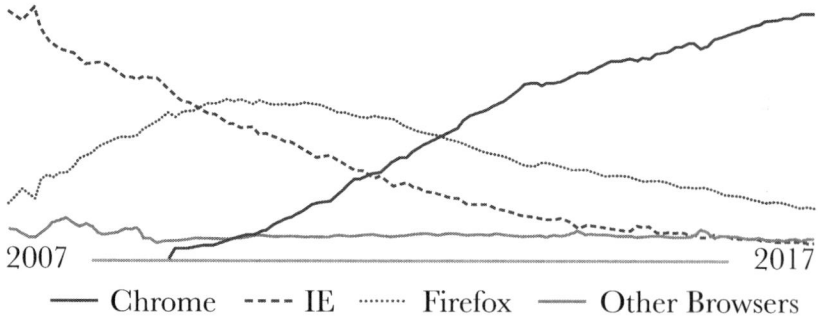

2007 ————————————————————————— 2017

—— Chrome    ---- IE    ········ Firefox    —— Other Browsers

---

[19] w3schools.com. (2017, February 16). *Browser Statistics*. Retreived from https://www.w3schools.com/browsers/

[20] "Usage share of operating systems." (2017, July 25). In Wikipedia, the Free Encyclopedia. Retrieved from https://en.wikipedia.org/w/index.php?title=Usage_share_of_operating_systems&oldid=792214448

Given that nearly everyone is using some version of a Google browser, the data collection machine is hard at work (whether users are logged in or not). Even without a Google account, Google engineers report collecting 57 data points from each Internet user accessing their search engine.[21] Google won't divulge what anonymous data is being collected; however, looking at what your browser is capable of reporting, it's reasonable to expect they know the following:

- Your approximate age, gender, and ethnicity: derived from your search history, browser, and device type.

- Affluence and education: derived from search history, location, use of slang, and frequency of typos in search. The cost of computer/mobile device being used. The use of keyboard shortcuts. The accuracy of the search; how often first page results are chosen.

- Environment: the weather where you are. The time of day.

- Your location: home, work, or a coffee shop.

- Your personal interests: derived from search history, browser themes, and ads you click on.

Google is not the only Internet company that collects user data. If you read just about any website's privacy policy, you'll find similar data collection practices. All of this information changes how the Internet responds to the user.

In 2010, regarding the power of individual targeting, the current CEO of Google, Eric Schmidt, said,

---

[21] Jenkins, H. (2010). "Google and the Search for the Future: The Web icon's CEO on the mobile computing revolution, the future of newspapers, and privacy in the digital age." The Wall Street Journal. August 14.

**THE TECHNOLOGY WILL BE SO GOOD IT WILL BE VERY HARD FOR PEOPLE TO WATCH OR CONSUME SOMETHING THAT HAS NOT IN SOME SENSE BEEN TAILORED FOR THEM.[22]**

Honestly, I have to admit, I am a fan of Google's apps and services. I love the convenience of Google knowing what I want, often before I do. Recently, I had a work meeting scheduled on my calendar at our counseling office. My office is at the production office, which is about four blocks away. I usually walk when traveling between offices. About 16 minutes before the meeting, I received a notification on my phone. I thought this was strange because all of my calendar events are set for a 10-minute notification. Taking a closer look at the notification I noticed that the navigation map showed my travel time as six minutes with a walking icon displayed. I realized that Google had been watching my travel patterns via the GPS in my phone and made the assumption that I was likely to walk to the meeting, adjusting my notification time to keep my day on schedule. Whether you find personalized information and free apps useful or not, when using the Internet it is important to understand that Internet companies want to know everything they possibly can about you. Why? They want to sell products and services to you.

---

[22] Ibid.

> IF YOU'RE NOT PAYING FOR IT, YOU'RE NOT THE CUSTOMER;
> YOU'RE THE PRODUCT BEING SOLD.
>
> ANDREW LEWIS[23]

If you are interested to know what Google specifically knows about you, visit www.google.com/dashboard.

## ANYTHING, ANYTIME, ANYWHERE _

The Internet is the global (Anywhere) network that allows electronic devices (Anytime) worldwide to connect and exchange information (Anything). Essentially, 1.3 zettabytes of data (and growing) allows the user to experience **anything** they want, convergence of all electronic devices allows the user the experience **anytime**, and four billion connections worldwide offers users the experience **anywhere**. Best of all, Anything, Anytime, Anywhere is virtually free! That is, if you don't mind being the product sold. I want to reiterate that the Internet is not inherently evil. As I pointed out earlier, there are many benefits our world has experienced as a result of the Internet. At the same time, it is critical to understand that its purpose and function is to market to the user.

When you combine the structure of Anything, Anytime, Anywhere with the prevalence of Internet pornography and targeted marketing, it's no wonder Generation Z is so severely addicted. It leads all of us who influence this generation—

---

[23] Lewis, A. (2010). "MetaFilter Community Weblog." Posted by blue_beetle (aka Andrew Lewis), August 26. Retrieved from http://www.metafilter.com/95152/Userdriven-discontent#3256046.

parents, school counselors and teachers, and others—to ask the question: knowing the design of the Internet, understanding how it is so much of our everyday lives, how do we teach our kids to use it responsibly? How do we balance isolating our kids from the world around us and not give into the sales pitch? I think this is the most practical modern-day application of Jesus' prayer from John 17 for His disciples:

> *My prayer is not that you take them out of the world*
> *but that you protect them from the evil one.*
> JOHN 17:15

Helping kids face the current challenges that the Internet poses starts with keeping them in the world, while at the same time, protecting them from the evil that is so prevalent. This means sheltering kids is not an option, neither is allowing them to access the Internet without boundaries. The ability to balance these extremes requires intentionality and awareness. Intentionally involved with all of the online activities that matter to kids. Awareness—paying attention to how the Internet works and how it is changing both our culture and the next generation.

# (1) CHAPTER RECAP
# HIGHLIGHTS FROM "A BRIEF HISTORY OF THE INTERNET"

**Who is Generation Z?** Generation Z can be identified by three main characteristics: 1) They do not understand a world without the Internet. 2) They do not know how to gain information without the Internet. 3) They do not know how to relate with other people outside of the Internet.

**The Internet is born.** The Internet was started by the United States (U.S.) Department of Defense. In the 1960s, the U.S. government started awarding contracts to universities and laboratories to develop ARPANET (Advanced Research Projects Agency Network). The goal of this project was to get computers in different locations to talk to each other via a universal network.

**What is convergence?** Convergence is the concept that every device is connected to the Internet and will uniquely communicate information to the user. Today, you can access the same Internet from your TV, laptop, tablet, phone, watch, game console, and many other devices.

**Internet Capability.** As of 1993, there was barely over half an exabyte (half a billion gigabytes) of data accessible on the Internet. Ten years later, in 2003, there was eight times the amount of data (nearly five exabytes) on the Internet. Over the next four years, into 2007, the Internet grew steadily to nineteen exabytes. Around 2007 things took off. In just nine years, the Internet grew by a factor of 70 times to a total of 1.2 zettabytes (1.3 trillion gigabytes).

**The Internet Marketplace.** The Internet companies that survived that dot-com bubble (Google, Netflix, eBay, Amazon), as well as newcomers to the market (Facebook, Twitter, YouTube, Reddit), saw that the Internet marketplace wasn't just a virtual version of a store that already existed. The market is not about retail: it's about advertising.

**Google wants to know you.** Given that nearly everyone is using some version of a Google browser, the data collection machine is hard at work (whether users are logged in or not). Even without a Google account, Google engineers report collecting 57 data points from each Internet user accessing their search engine.

**Anything, Anytime, Anywhere.** The Internet is the global (Anywhere) network that allows electronic devices (Anytime) worldwide to connect and exchange information (Anything). Essentially, 1.3 zettabytes of data (and growing) allows the user to experience anything they want, convergence of all electronic devices allows the user the experience anytime, and four billion connections worldwide offers users the experience anywhere.

**So what's the problem?** When you combine the structure of Anything, Anytime, Anywhere with the prevalence of Internet pornography and targeted marketing, it's no wonder Generation Z is so severely addicted.

# THE INTERNET KNOWS KIDS

Have you ever bought a house? Rented a car? Signed up for a credit card? If you are an average American adult, there's a good chance that you said yes to one of those questions. There is also an equally good chance that when buying a house, renting a car, or obtaining a credit card you were asked to agree to a ridiculously long set of conditions and terms of agreement, written in the smallest font possible, by a group of lawyers that clearly had a very difficult childhood.

I remember the first house that my wife and I purchased. I kept thinking: *Wow, there is this really nice bank that is going to loan us more money than I make in a year to purchase a house. What a nice bank!* On the day of signing for our mortgage, my perspective of the friendly bank people changed. I think it happened when signing page 23 of 174 of our paperwork. I quickly realized that the now "not so nice bank people" wanted two things in exchange for letting me use their money to buy a house: one, about four times the amount they loaned me to be repaid; two, if anything went wrong with the deal, it was pretty much my fault and I was on the hook for it.

Clearly, the bank had way more experience with mortgages than I did. At some point amid all of the "sign here," "initial this," and "date that," I became overwhelmed. I pretty much checked out and just started signing wherever I was told. Our mortgage broker, would say, "And this document says that in the event of... blah, blah, blah, you agree to...blah, blah, blah," and I responded with, "Okay, sounds good," while signing on the dotted line.

Years later, I'm happy to say that, so far, with every house, credit card, rental car, and everything else that required me to sign a lengthy contract, none of the fine print has happened...yet. One thing is pretty clear in looking at a contract of this nature: the organization offering the contract is serious about things going according to plan and getting what they want out of you.

In the last chapter, we looked at how Internet companies specifically target users for personal information so they can market to the individual. Much like the bank that let me borrow money to purchase my house, Internet companies are serious about getting what they want out of you.

In contrast to banks, Internet companies are much more subtle in their approach to getting you to agree to their terms and conditions. Instead of bringing you a ream of paper full of legalese to sign, they usually give you a little message on the screen with a box to check that says something like "I have read and agree to the privacy policy." The vast majority of users never even open the link to the privacy policy to which they agree. Those who have ever clicked the link to read these agreements is most definitely sorry they did.

## THE PRIVACY POLICY _

What is a privacy policy and why is it important to an Internet company? Simply put, it is an agreement with the user stating what data about the user can be collected and how they can use that data. Much like a mortgage contract, the terms can quickly become complex and detailed.

A 2012 study conducted by Carnegie Mellon researchers reviewed the top 75 Internet sites' privacy policies their users were required to sign.[24] They found that the average policy contained 2,514 words. They looked at how many of these policies the average Internet user is likely to encounter in the course of a year's worth of Internet use. When they asked the participants to not only read the policies, but also understand them to the point they could pass a simple reading comprehension test, the researchers were stunned by the results. The data revealed that it would take 25 days—more than 600 hours or 76 eight-hour workdays—to read and comprehend all of the policies that the average user was likely to encounter in the course of a year. In a *TIME* news article reporting on the study, contributor Keith Wagstaff made the following observation about the amount of time necessary to understand privacy policies:

THAT NUMBER SOUNDS RIDICULOUS BECAUSE NOBODY ACTUALLY SPENDS THAT MUCH TIME READING ALL OF THE PRIVACY POLICIES THAT THEY ENCOUNTER ON THE INTERNET— WHICH, OF COURSE, IS THE POINT. RIGHT NOW, THE RESPONSIBILITY IS ON THE USER; LAWYERS MAKE SURE THE FACEBOOKS OF THE WORLD HAVE ALL OF THEIR BASES COVERED.

---

[24] Wagstaff, K. (2012). "You'd Need 76 Work Days to Read All Your Privacy Policies Each Year." Time Inc. March 6. Retrieved from http://techland.time.com/2012/03/06/youd-need-76-work-days-to-read-all-your-privacy-policies-each-year/

Do you have 76 spare work days to read over privacy agreements? I didn't think so. Something isn't quite right with how the whole system works and—while not a panacea—shifting more of the responsibility to the websites who want to profit off your data might be a good way to start fixing it.

Unfortunately, since the publication of that article in 2012, things have not improved. Internet companies have virtually no oversight pressure to make their privacy policies readable, and users generally have no interest in reading them. Internet companies can pretty much put anything into a privacy policy without discouraging users from signing up for their services. One of Apple's previous agreements for their iTunes application stated that they *"expressly forbid you from using iTunes to create missiles and biological, chemical, or nuclear weapons."*[25]

The developers at PC Pitstop, a computer diagnostics application provider, were apparently curious to find out if anyone ever read their application's terms of use.[26] They temporarily added the following clause to their policy: *"A special consideration, which may include financial compensation, will be awarded to a limited number of authorized licensees to read this section of the license agreement and contact PC Pitstop at consideration@ pcpitstop.com. This offer can be withdrawn at any time."* PC Pitstop was good to their word issuing a $1,000 check to the first person who contacted them about the special clause. Not surprisingly, it took five months and more than 3,000 sales before the first person sent an email asking about the clause.

---

[25] Hoffman, C. (2012). "10 Ridiculous EULA Clauses That You May Have Already Agreed To." MakeUseOf. April 23. Retrieved from http://www.makeuseof.com/tag/10-ridiculous-eula-clauses-agreed/

[26] The Pit Crew (2012). "It Pays To Read License Agreements (7 Years Later)." PC Pitstop TechTalk. June 12. Retrieved from http://techtalk.pcpitstop.com/2012/06/12/it-pays-to-read-license-agreements-7-years-later/

Although the previous two examples are a bit comical, they do a good job of making the point that Internet companies pretty much have free rein to do whatever they choose with users' data. In a more practical application not involving nuclear weapons or cash prizes, Google's Chrome browser privacy policy states, *"You give Google a perpetual, irrevocable, worldwide, royalty-free, and non-exclusive license to reproduce, adapt, modify, translate, publish, publicly perform, publicly display and distribute any Content which you submit, post or display on or through, the Services."*[27] When doing the research for this chapter, this particular policy gave me pause for concern since I'm using my Google Chromebook, with Chrome browser, in Google Docs to write this book. I'm a little worried that Google might own the copyrights to this book. Maybe I should give my lawyer a call!

So if no one reads the privacy policies and Internet companies are likely to put literally any condition in them, what is the point of bringing this up? Well, first, let me say I'm not encouraging anyone to waste 600 plus hours of their lives, per year, reading boring legal gibberish. I'm also not trying to discourage Internet use. As stated in the last chapter, avoiding Internet use is not a reasonable option for Generation Z. My goal is to answer the question: What do Internet companies know about me and what is the net effect of that information?

---

[27] Hoffman, C. (2012). "10 Ridiculous EULA Clauses That You May Have Already Agreed To." MakeUseOf. April 23. Retrieved from http://www.makeuseof.com/tag/10-ridiculous-eula-clauses-agreed/

# THE TRUTH OF ADVERTISING _

## HALF THE MONEY I SPEND ON ADVERTISING IS WASTED. THE PROBLEM IS I DON'T KNOW WHICH HALF.

LORD LEVERHULME[28]

According to TechCrunch, the global advertising market is estimated at more than $500 billion annually.[29] You can only imagine how competitive a market of that size is and the importance for advertisers to make every dollar count. In October of 2000, Google launched AdWords, an entirely new concept in advertising.[30] Advertisers would choose key search words that best described their products and services. When a user would request a Google search, the AdWords listings would be placed at the very top of the search results. The only time that the companies using the AdWords service paid for the ad was when someone clicked on the link to their website. The AdWords service was fundamentally different from any other before offered mass-market strategy.

If you look at television or print media, the very best you could hope for is targeting a broad demographic based on the show or article for which you were purchasing ad space. This worked well for some products; beer commercials clearly belonged in the Super Bowl, Lego, Mattel, and Hasbro purchased

---

[28] Osborne, M. (2016). *Stop Advertising, Start Branding: How to Build the Brand that Will Build Your Business*. Kibworth Beauchamp, Leicester: Troubador Publishing.

[29] Lunden, I. (2013). "Digital Ads Will Be 22% of All U.S. Ad Spend In 2013, Mobile Ads 3.7%; Total Global Ad Spend In 2013 $503B." TechCrunch. September 30. Retrieved from https://www.reference.com/business-finance/big-advertising-industry-78c66e17c3dc5cee

[30] AdWords. (2017, July 23). In Wikipedia, the Free Encyclopedia. Retrieved from https://en.wikipedia.org/w/index.php?title=AdWords&oldid=791944619

Saturday morning cartoon spots, while your local grocery store put coupons in the Sunday paper for you to clip.

The problem was that for many businesses the demographic was less obvious. Spending millions of dollars on ads was not profitable or even feasible to businesses that couldn't say exactly what show their customers were likely to watch or what print article they were likely to read. Google AdWords provided businesses with customers who were clearly looking for that business's exact product or service by the submission of the user's search. Not only that, but AdWords customers only paid when a potential customer clicked the ad link and visited their site.

Given that Google processes 3.5 billion searches per day, even the most obscure businesses were almost guaranteed to have customers visit their site. When launched, AdWords was truly a never-seen-before type of advertisement. Businesses could literally purchase potential customers. Looking at the growth of AdWords over the last 15 years you get a clear sense of its effectiveness. In just 15 years, nearly 1,000 percent growth.[31]

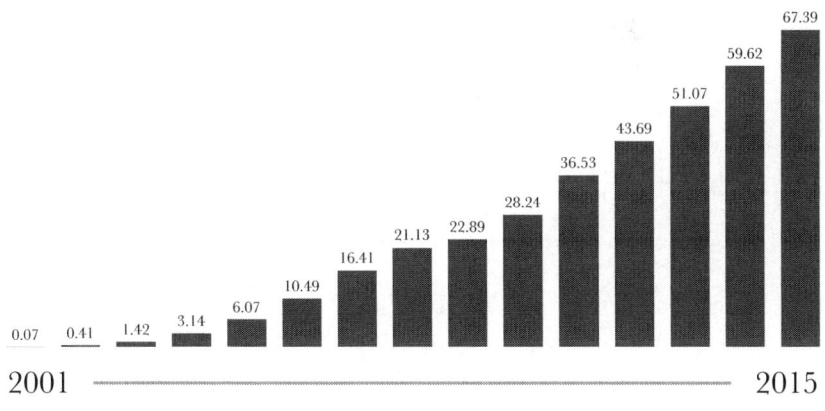

2001 —————————————————————————————— 2015

---

[31] Statista Inc. "Google's ad revenue from 2001 to 2015 (in billion U.S. Dollars)." Retrieved from http://www.statista.com/statistics/266249/advertising-revenue-of-google/

Google AdWords was really just the start of targeted marketing. Google started offering many other services to their users for free to gain even more personal information. After observing Google's initial success, virtually every other Internet company rewrote their privacy policy and began to collect massive amounts of data on all their users.

## I THINK I'M BEING FOLLOWED! _

Now that Google had shown how lucrative it was to offer services in exchange for user data, there was almost no limit to what a developer would do to collect data. Most services like Twitter, Facebook, and YouTube launched without ads. They spent several years developing their technology and gaining users. Operating on venture capital as start-ups, the one and only goal of these services was to provide a unique service that would attract a massive user base and collect enormous amounts of data about users.

All of these companies eventually began to run ads on their sites specifically targeting their users. Facebook built their user base for eight years before placing ads in the news feed. YouTube and Twitter followed the same formula with video ads and sponsored tweets. This formula eventually became the standard start-up path for virtually every developer starting a new Internet company.

## ⊛ INTERNET STARTUP 101:

1. Come up with a useful app that leverages the Internet's power of Anything, Anytime, Anywhere to create a captivating experience for the user.

2. Embed a social aspect to draw not only interested users but also their friends.

3. Offer free accounts with open-ended privacy policies.

4. Monetize the site or application with targeted ads.

5. Sell the service on the stock market with an exorbitant IPO—Initial Public Offering.

6. Retire at age 23!

Along with the mass collection of data in the early 2000s, Internet companies started customizing the user experience. I touched on this briefly in the last chapter with Google's former CEO Eric Schmidt's quote about tailored search results. This concept of the Internet knowing you—and your kids—so well that it attempts to predict with surprising accuracy what you want is extremely powerful. Google started playing with the idea of personalized search in 2004, and by 2005 it was a standard feature in all Google searches.[32] Personalized search is almost undetectable to users in their daily online searches. It can only be identified in comparison to someone else's online profile. If you want to see it in action, all you need is a friend who has a different interest, background, location, or perspective in one or more areas.

While writing this chapter I decided to give it a try. I confiscated my wife's laptop. Knowing she and I have many things in common—religious beliefs, close in age, political views, similar social perspectives, ideas on parenting, and probably most importantly location (the same Internet connection)—I realized this might be tricky to see. I wasn't even sure if coming from the same Internet connection Google could discern the difference between our two laptops.

---

[32] "Google Personalized Search." (2017, July 10). In Wikipedia, the Free Encyclopedia. Retrieved from https://en.wikipedia.org/wiki/Google_Personalized_Search

I tried to think of at least two specific differences and the first two that came to mind were cars and homeschool. I am a bit of a car enthusiast; I love reading about the latest, greatest automotive technology, especially exotic cars. For elementary and middle school we chose to homeschool our kids. My wife has played a significant role in both kids' education, ordering materials, as well as teaching at and directing our co-op. I decided to enter the same two searches on our two laptops: "cars" and "homeschool."

When I put in the search for "cars" there were some similarities; however, many more differences:

| MY RESULTS | MY WIFE'S RESULTS |
|---|---|
| **⊙ LINKS** | |
| • News article on the ethics of autonomous cars | • Disney Cars home page |
| • Cnet - road show | • Edmunds reviews |
| • Digitaltrends.com article top 10 supercars | • Cars IMDB (movie review) |
| **⊙ PICTURES** | |
| • Bugatti Veyron | • Toyota Sienna |
| • McLaren P1 | • Nissan Leaf |
| • Porsche 818 | • BMW i3 |
| • Ferrari LaFerrari | • Kia Optima |

Clearly Google knows I have spent a good deal of time online lusting after supercars. Google also figured that my wife's only interest in cars was Disney movies and getting the kids from point A to point B in the safest, greenest vehicle possible. When I searched for "homeschool" the differences were even more stark:

| MY RESULTS | MY WIFE'S RESULTS |
|---|---|
| **❯ LINKS** | |
| • homeschool.com<br>• Wikipedia: Homeschool<br>• Local homeschool co-op site | • discountschoolsupply.com<br>• calverteducation.com (online academy)<br>• icademy.com (online academy) |
| **❯ PICTURES** | |
| • Various clipart and pictures of homeschoolers | • None on the first page of results |

Google knows that my wife is an active homeschool mom who is likely to buy supplies or enroll her kids in an online academy. Google also isn't so sure that I know anything about homeschooling, therefore offering me basic information about homeschooling, as well as some pictures of what it looks like.

Although this customized data is very useful and convenient, there are huge side effects, especially for a kid's developing brain.

Facebook has taken the art of custom data to an entirely new level. The main page of Facebook's interface is the news feed.[33] This is where all of your friends, pages you like, groups

---

[33] Facebook Help Center. "How News Feed Works." Retrieved from https://www.facebook.com/help/327131014036297/

you join, and, of course, paid advertisement posts are displayed. Given the number of friends, pages, and groups the average user is connected to, there are an estimated 10,000 posts generated each day for each user's news feed, not including paid ad posts. This would be way more information than any reasonable user would want to sift through, which is why Facebook has a feed algorithm to sort the information for you. Here is how Facebook describes this process:

> THE STORIES THAT SHOW IN YOUR NEWS FEED ARE INFLUENCED BY YOUR CONNECTIONS AND ACTIVITY ON FACEBOOK. THIS HELPS YOU TO SEE MORE STORIES THAT INTEREST YOU FROM FRIENDS YOU INTERACT WITH THE MOST. THE NUMBER OF COMMENTS AND LIKES A POST RECEIVES AND WHAT KIND OF STORY IT IS.

No one outside of Facebook knows exactly how their feed algorithms work, and no one working at Facebook is allowed to talk about how they work. What is clear is that even though we choose who we are friends with, Facebook determines which ones are important to us. When asked about the relevance of data on Facebook for its users, CEO Mark Zuckerberg said: *"A squirrel dying in front of your house may be more relevant to your interests right now than people dying in Africa."*[34] Zuckerberg's comment draws attention to a fairly terrifying trend being seen among Internet users, especially Gen Z users.

---

[34] Pariser, E. (2011). "When the Internet Thinks It Knows You." The New York Times. May 22. Retrieved from http://www.nytimes.com/2011/05/23/opinion/23pariser.html

## PORNOGRAPHY ISN'T THE GREATEST THREAT TO KIDS ON THE INTERNET _

When considering that Google is working very hard to return results that are specifically tailored to kids, and Facebook's algorithms are trying to always display the posts it believes kids are most likely to respond to—with a like, share, or comment— you begin to see a very unnatural environment emerging. These are only two examples of Internet companies using personal data to curtail the Internet for the benefit of advertising. Most news and media organizations, online stores, streaming data services, and just about every other type of Internet service collects data and applies data and customizes their site for the individual user's experience.

What causes customers to buy on impulse? The Internet capitalizes on the most impulsive version of you. According to research, the type of advertising that may have the greatest effect on your brain, behavior, and impulse control may be counterintuitive.[35] Collaborative research at the University of California and George Washington University focused on two types of advertisements: logical persuasion (LP) and non-rational influence (NI). LP advertising highlights the product's features, such as, Hydro Flask: keeps cold up to 24 hours. NI advertising contains images or content completely unrelated to the product, displaying a fun, exciting, or sexy scene to sell office supplies.

Participants looked at advertising images while researchers monitored the electrical brain activity using electroencephalography (EEG). The results are surprising.

---

[35] Melina, R. (2011). "How Advertisements Seduce Your Brain." Live Science. September 23. Retrieved from https://www.livescience.com/16169-advertisements-seduce-brain.html

When participants looked at the LP ads, the regions of the brain responsible for decision-making and emotional processing—the orbitofrontal and anterior cingulate regions, and the amygdala and hippocampus of the limbic system—showed significantly higher levels of activity. These areas of the brain are instrumental in controlling impulsive behaviors, such as impulse spending. However, when participants observed the NI ads, these areas of the brain showed less activity comparatively. The results indicate that the lower levels of brain activity—indicative of less behavioral inhibition—from the NI advertisements could affect an individual's restraint when it comes to buying.

What does this have to do with kids? The answer lies in their brain development, or lack of brain development. The prefrontal cortex—the area of the brain directly behind the forehead—is vital to one's ability to control their behavior, make decisions and plan, and understand or relate to others.[36] This area of the brain is the last to develop, sometime during the mid-twenties.

However, it is during the early stages of brain development that the limbic system is developed—the area of the brain that is highly responsive to the neurotransmitter dopamine, and responsible for emotional expression, reward, and memory.[37] Although many other variables are at play during this stage of development, the adolescent brain, at a fundamental level, is out of balance. The limbic system is thriving, searching for novelty and stimulation, while the prefrontal cortex is inhibited by a lack of development.

---

[36] Loveday, C. (2016). *The Secret World of the Brain: What it does, how it works, and how it affects behavior.* New York, NY: Metro Books.

[37] Abrahams, P. (2015). *How the Brain Works: Understanding Brain Functions, Thought, and Personality.* New York, NY: Bright Star Publishing Plc.

Today, even though teenagers are the leading experts on technology and the most knowledgeable users of the Internet, they are also the most vulnerable.[38] Whether a teen is outgoing and popular or shy and introverted, the Internet offers a virtual social landscape where it is easier to connect with people. For many adolescents, the anonymity of their online experience becomes more pleasurable, more rewarding, and more real than their offline existence. For the first time historically, Generation Z is exposed to numerous digital distractions and therefore more susceptible to its influence. Dr. Frances Jensen describes it this way:

> THE CASCADE OF NEUROPROCESSES THAT KICKS OFF THE BRAIN'S REWARD CIRCUITRY AND THE RUSH OF THE PLEASURE CHEMICAL DOPAMINE CAN BE SO TRIGGERED JUST AS EASILY BY THE RELEASE OF THE LATEST IPHONE AS BY ALCOHOL, POT, SEX, OR A FAST CAR.[39]

For many unsuspecting teens, the Internet, like drug use, involves the same reward center of the brain—in some ways, making technology as influential and addictive as drugs. There is evidence to suggest that excessive Internet use among adolescents contributes to mood disturbances, depression, poor academic performance, and an inability to manage their online time. They become addicted to the Internet. In 2009, reSTART opened their doors as one of the first inpatient treatment programs for treating problematic and addictive digital media use.[40] Using an

---

[38] Jensen, F. & Ellis Nutt, A. (2015). *The Teenage Brain: A Neuroscientist's Survival Guide to Raising Adolescents and Young Adults.* New York, NY: HarperCollins Publishers.

[39] Ibid. 206.

[40] reSTART. Retrieved from https://netaddictionrecovery.com/

evidence-based approach, they address the underlying factors that result in Internet addictive behaviors, exhibited by symptoms of anxiety, depression, increasing distractibility, social isolation, physical deterioration, and sleep disturbances.

What many people don't understand is that the compulsive need to be digitally connected is both behavioral and biochemical.[41] The brain becomes conditioned to every text, ring, and ping—any noise that a smartphone makes to announce the opportunity for connection, resulting in a surge of excitement and a release of dopamine in the brain. If the sound alone wasn't enough, the opening of the message is like receiving a digital gift, producing the reward of more dopamine in the brain. Whether they know it or not, they're hooked.

Here's where this all comes together. Many Internet companies are using "buzz or street marketing" to advertise their product, not only to their young users, but in many ways, taking advantage of this technologically savvy generation and their social networking dependency.[42] Internet companies rely on their young users to circulate the latest-and-greatest music, clothes, beverages, hot spots, and more via Facebook, YouTube, and Twitter. Their lack of impulse control coupled with their need for novelty and stimulation provides the catalyst by which the teen brain becomes addicted to the Internet. And remember, the Internet, which is all about collecting data on its users, knows kids.

Although many would say that pornography is a pandemic for Gen Z, I think it is much more accurate to say that pornography

---

[41] Jensen, F. & Ellis Nutt, A. (2015). *The Teenage Brain: A Neuroscientist's Survival Guide to Raising Adolescents and Young Adults*. New York, NY: HarperCollins Publishers.

[42] MediaSmarts. "How Marketers Target Kids." Retrieved from http://mediasmarts.ca/digital-media-literacy/media-issues/marketing-consumerism/how-marketers-target-kids

is a symptom of an Internet addiction pandemic. When impulse control is impaired and a need for novelty and stimulation is developed, widespread use of pornography is kind of…a no-brainer (pun intended).

You may be saying, "Okay, I'm officially terrified that the Internet has or will soon irreparably mess up my kids! What can I, as a parent, grandparent, school counselor, teacher, or church leader, do?" As a follower of Christ there is good news. Taking a look at scripture gives great insight and perspective to how we can positively influence the current generation.

## NOTHING NEW UNDER THE SUN MAINFRAME _

Although Internet companies like Google and Facebook may have found a new spin on marketing, we have been here before. Solomon, the wisest king of the Old Testament writes: "What has been will be again, what has been done will be done again; there is nothing new under the sun" (Ecclesiastes 1:9).

In the New Testament Paul writes to the Corinthians: "No temptation has overtaken you except what is common to mankind" (1 Corinthians 10:13). At the end of the day, the Internet companies are exchanging the allure of self-focus idolatry for sales. Again, I'm not saying that any convenience or service the Internet provides is evil; however, when you get to the point where brain function is severely altered, it's probably a good time to take two steps back.

The important question is: are you, the user, aware of the effects? A couple of years ago, my son was using his daily allotment of screen time to play Minecraft (a virtual reality building game—think of digital Legos). He had been playing for about 30 minutes when my wife asked him to take out the recycling.

Without even taking his eyes off of the screen he snapped back, "Mom, not now! I'm busy." It was at this point the computer went off and we had a discussion about how people in the real world (e.g. Mom) are much more important than Steve (the main protagonist in the game). My son is incredibly creative, with a mind for creative problem-solving. Minecraft is a great learning experience that stimulates his young engineering mind; however, not at the cost of relationship. It is so easy to become immersed in the digital landscape of our modern world that it's often difficult to see its effects.

In 2014, *TIME* magazine released an article entitled "Most Americans Don't Understand How the Internet Works."[43] The report reviewed a study by the Pew Research Center that basically says, although nearly every American uses the Internet on a daily basis, very few users know how it works or even how it came into existence. This means that all of the "your brain on the Internet" studies are conducted on a population of people who don't understand how the Internet works. You might be thinking, *No wonder our brains are messed up; most people don't know they are lab rats in the Google/Facebook marketing experiment!*

Taking another look at the automobile analogy from chapter 0, you could draw the conclusion that this is normal human behavior. I would imagine that of the billion-plus drivers in the world, most would not pass a test on the workings of an internal combustion engine, or a transmission, or hydraulic brakes. Most people don't even know the three factors that contribute to hydroplaning: speed, water, and tire tread. Don't feel bad, I didn't know that one either. I Googled it. Darn, I'm probably

---

[43]  Linshi, J. (2014). Study: "Most Americans Don't Understand How the Internet Works." Time Inc. http://time.com/3602105/internet-knowledge-test-pew/

going to see tire ads on my Facebook feed for the next week. Even without all of this important information, every day drivers busily hop into their cars without checking the tread depth on their tires or inspecting the brake fluid reservoir. Why? We are comfortable driving without considering the risk of operating a vehicle that may not be in the best shape. It isn't until we slam on the brakes at 60 mph, hoping that we don't rear-end the car in front of us, that we think, *Huh, I wonder how long it's been since I had the brakes serviced?*

Most Internet users don't evaluate their Internet use until they end up in a place, or participate in a behavior, they never wanted. Just like in driver's education: knowledge and self-evaluation put into action is a powerful combination. Reading this book will give you the insight to the inner workings of the Internet, as well as behavioral clues to pay attention to when evaluating online behavior. I believe it is possible to be in the Internet without being of the Internet. It requires being present, aware, and willing to make change.

## THE DIGITAL-GENERATIONAL CURSE

The action part of the equation is the toughest and most important part. Whether it's your kids, a student, or family member, those who you disciple will never be farther down the road than you are. If you're struggling with pornography or other unhealthy online behavior, it's a pretty good chance that those who follow you, will be as well. In Exodus Moses declares the danger of idolatry to the Israelites:

*You shall not bow down to them or worship them; for I, the LORD your God, am a jealous God, punishing the children for the sin of the parents to the third and fourth generation of those who hate me, but showing love to a thousand generations of those who love me and keep my commandments.*

EXODUS 20:56

It's interesting to see this scripture in action. Working at Pure Desire, I've lost count of the number of people who have shared their story of sexual addiction and identified the sin of their parents being passed down. "I was looking through the browser history on my dad's computer when I first found porn" or "I was getting links and pop-ups to porn sites. I wasn't even looking for anything inappropriate." It's important to realize that when our kids use our computer or Internet connection, the Internet will return the most impulsive version of their parents too.

## CHAPTER RECAP
2
# HIGHLIGHTS FROM "THE INTERNET KNOWS KIDS"

**The Privacy Policy.** Simply put, a privacy policy is an agreement with the user stating what data about the user can be collected and how they can use that data. Much like a mortgage contract, the terms can quickly become complex and detailed.

**What is AdWords?** In October of 2000, Google launched AdWords; an entirely new concept in advertising. Advertisers would choose key search words that best described their products and services. When a user would request a Google search, the AdWords listings would be placed at the very top of the search results.

**Who's using who?** Operating on venture capital as start-ups, the one and only goal of these services was to provide a unique service that would attract a massive user base and collect enormous amounts of data about users. Each of these companies eventually began to run ads on their sites specifically targeting their users.

**Google knows you personally.** Google started playing with the idea of personalized search in 2004, and by 2005 it was a standard feature in all Google searches. Personalized search is almost undetectable to users in their daily online searches. It can only be identified in comparison to someone else's online profile.

**The Greatest Threat on the Internet.** When considering that Google is working very hard to return results that are specifically tailored to kids, and Facebook's algorithms are trying to always display the posts it believes kids are most likely to respond to—with a like, share, or comment—you begin to see a very unnatural environment emerging.

**Brain Development.** What does this have to do with kids? The answer lies in their brain development, or lack of brain development. Although many other variables are at play during this stage of development, the adolescent brain, at a fundamental level, is out of balance.

**The Teen Brain and the Internet.** Today, even though teenagers are the leading experts on technology and the most knowledgeable users of the Internet, they are also the most vulnerable. Whether a teen is outgoing and popular or shy and introverted, the Internet offers a virtual social landscape where it is easier to connect with people.

**Internet Addiction.** For many unsuspecting teens, the Internet, like drug use, involves the same reward center of the brain—in some ways, making technology as influential and addictive as drugs. There is evidence to suggest that excessive Internet use among adolescents contributes to mood disturbances, depression, poor academic performance, and an inability to manage their online time.

**The Digital-Generation Curse.** It's important to realize that when our kids use our computer or Internet connection, the Internet will return the most impulsive version of their parents too. If you are struggling with pornography or other unhealthy online behavior, it's a pretty good chance that those who follow you, will be as well.

# INTERNET ADDICTION– IT'S A PROCESS

Have you ever started a big project and thought, *How difficult could it be?* only to find out it was extremely difficult? Maybe it was a home improvement project you saw on a TV remodel show and thought, *Hey, I can do that!* Perhaps you had a plan to lose that extra 10 pounds, or a goal of running a half marathon thinking, *Lots of people do this, why can't I?* Maybe you wanted to create a work-from-home start-up business to generate a little extra income, only to find that it was mostly extra work and little income. Maybe someone encouraged you to write a book about helping the current generation learn how to use the Internet responsibly, and you thought, *I know a lot about the Internet—this will be a cinch!* I'm finding that last one is much harder than it sounds, at least so far; I'll keep you posted.

## HOW DIFFICULT COULD IT BE? _

About seven years ago, I took on a seemingly trivial task only to find it was anything but trivial. As a matter of fact, in many ways, I'm still working on it.

One of the drawbacks of moving from a laser engineer to a nonprofit director is that I tend to sit at the desk quite a bit more. In my 17 years of high-tech work, I always seemed to be on my feet. I had an office and there were times that I spent the day at my desk, but it was pretty rare. Most of the time I was out on the production floor inspecting work, in the maintenance shop machining parts for a new build, or crammed in a machine trying to fix the encoder of a variable optical aperture. Seriously, why do they put the part of a laser that breaks the most in the hardest place to reach? It doesn't even have to be a laser. I think that's a universal law of mechanics: This part is likely to break frequently. Okay, let's make sure it's really hard to get to.

Anyway, about a year into working at Pure Desire, I was sitting at my desk trying to figure out a new business plan for our resources and hit a wall. I sat back in my chair, stretched a bit then slumped down with my arms by my side. Looking down I noticed something rather strange. My legs had disappeared! Well, actually, I just couldn't see them. My stomach was blocking my view. I thought to myself, "Wow! I've put on some weight."

When I got home from work that evening I scoured the bathroom cabinets in search of the scale. Ah, behind the first aid kit. There it is! I quickly closed the bathroom door, locked it, set the scale on the floor next to the tub and then took two steps back. I felt like a kid in the principal's office, terrified to step forward and accept my fate. I took a deep breath, then slowly, carefully put one foot on the scale, then the next. The scale began to spin. I held my breath, sucked in my stomach, and closed my eyes (like that was going to help). After a few seconds, I opened one eye, and then the other. The scale read: 218 pounds. WHAT! That can't be right! I quickly proceeded to take off my shoes, thinking, *I know these Doc Martens have thick soles, but 218 pounds? That's ridiculous.* I weighed myself again—216 pounds. *It must be the belt!* So off went the belt. Still 216. Then the pants, shirt, socks, and watch; finally, I found myself in my bathroom with the door locked, standing in my underwear on a scale that read 214 pounds.

With a labored sigh I got dressed and went into my office. I sat down at the computer and Googled "BMI calculator." I typed in 5 foot 8 inches, 214 pounds. (I'm actually 5 foot 7½ inches, but this seemed like a really good time to round up.) The calculator displayed "BMI-33: Obese." Obese? I leaned in to look closer at the screen, as if it was going to change. I noticed that not only was I in the obese range, I was smack dab in the middle. I wasn't slightly obese. I was average-obese, well in the range; like I'd been there a while, really settled in, and made myself comfortable.

In all of my 36 years, I had never identified with being obese. Sure, I had been overweight, but obese? That wasn't me. No, I was the guy who just had a few pounds to lose. Obese people were on those reality shows taking desperate measures to lose 200 pounds. Obese people had no self-control, or some genetic metabolic disorder. I wasn't one of those people, or so I thought. Although, I didn't have 200 pounds to lose or a genetic disorder, when it came to food, I was out of control. I didn't know that at the time; all I knew was that I had just received an enormous dose of reality and something had to change.

## REALITY AT ALL COSTS

Reality is a funny thing. Looking back at my life, prior to the day I stood on the bathroom scale in my underwear, stunned and bewildered, I had never thought of myself as someone who was out of touch with reality. Scott Peck, psychiatrist and author says, "Mental health is a commitment to reality at all costs."[44] A couple weeks after the bathroom scale incident, I read that quote while completing my *Seven Pillars of Freedom* weekly homework. The further I traveled in my journey of becoming a healthier me, the more I understood Peck's words. When I made the decision that losing weight was not an option, I would have identified **reality at all costs** this way: "I'm obese. That's reality. I didn't know it before, but I know it now; and darn it, I'm buckling down and fixing it!"

Today, I would describe it much differently. **Reality at all costs** is not a mantra of extreme commitment or will power, but a state of mind—of being present and aware. **Reality at all costs** is about knowing the truth and being willing to admit where my behavior does not match. Unlike fantasy, which is knowing the truth and deciding to ignore it. Now, I'm happy to report that the bathroom scale and I have a much better relationship. As of this morning, I weigh 151 pounds and my BMI has been classified as "normal" for the last two years.

Part of my job at Pure Desire includes traveling to events across the United States. I frequently meet friends connected to the ministry that I haven't seen since 30, 40, or even 60 pounds ago. Every time I meet friends I haven't seen in a while, the conversation is always the same. At first it was a bit awkward, but now it's almost comical.

It goes something like this: "Bryan? Is that you? I almost didn't recognize you. Have you lost weight?"

I usually respond with, "Yeah, it's me. Yep, 65 pounds. It's so good to see you again!"

---

[44] Peck, S. (1978). *The Road Less Traveled: A New Psychology of Love, Traditional Values, and Spiritual Growth.* New York, NY: Simon & Schuster.

Then with a look of sheer amazement, as if they had just watched me pull off the coolest magic trick of all time, they ask the question that everyone asks: "How did you do it?"

Now, this is the hard part because I feel like I'm about to ruin the coolest magic trick of all time. Not by telling them how I did it, but even worse, telling them that it's not really a magic trick at all. My response is always the same.

I say these three simple words "diet and exercise" and instantly all of the joy and amusement is sucked right out of the conversation, replaced with the sobering response of, "Oh right…diet and exercise…of course." It was the answer they knew was coming, but hoping that I wouldn't say it.

Although diet and exercise is an accurate answer, it is incomplete. It doesn't really explain why I'm statistically in a small minority of the 5 percent of people who have lost weight and managed to keep it off for 5 years.[45] If I have the opportunity to spend some time with someone I haven't seen in a while and really share my story, I can give a much better answer. I usually say something like: "I thought losing weight would be an easy thing to do. I remember thinking a lot of people do it; how hard could it be?" Then I tell them about **reality at all costs**.

The truth is that when I started dieting I was only committed to reality at the extremely high cost of obesity. I had no idea that I would be facing some very real and very serious medical conditions if change did not occur.[46]

- Heart disease
- Diabetes
- Gallstones
- Sleep apnea
- Stroke
- Cancer
- Osteoarthritis
- Asthma
- High blood pressure
- Gallbladder disease
- Gout

[45] The Council on Size and Weight Discrimination. (2011, July 18). "Statics on Weight Discrimination: A Waste of Talent." Retrieved from http://cswd.org/statistics-2

[46] DerSarkissian, C. (2016). "Health Risks Linked to Obesity." Retrieved from http://www.webmd.com/diet/obesity/obesity-health-risks

Although obesity and the associated diseases clearly got my attention, there were many other lower cost reality checks I completely missed. It wasn't as if one day I was slightly overweight and the next day I was obese. Over a year's time, there was a progression in my thinking and actions where I was ignoring the reality and living out my fantasy. I lied to myself and others. I believed that even though at my new job I sat at my desk all day, I didn't need to be active outside of work. That I could eat comfort food to feel at peace or better about myself. That I could binge eat to numb out and avoid the pressure created by my workaholism. Oh yeah, I found out that I was a workaholic too. That came with a whole other realm of fantasy and problems. My comorbidity[47] (multiple addictions that exist together—food and work in my case) was generating a vicious binge-purge cycle with the root of people-pleasing; driven by my wounds from my past where I was told, "You aren't good enough, or smart enough for people to like you." At work, I would say "yes" to everything I was asked to do to make everyone like me.

This created a ridiculous amount of work that I attempted to accomplish to gain acceptance. All the while, even when I was praised for my work, I felt empty. I begin to believe that people only liked me if I could give them what they wanted. This emptiness drove me to crave high-calorie, high-fat foods to feel comforted. Eventually, I would work so hard to please everyone and either fail or feel so exhausted that I just didn't want to feel any more. When I hit exhaustion, I would binge-eat to numb out and not feel anything.

---

[47] NIDA. (2011, March 1). "Comorbidity: Addiction and Other Mental Disorders." Retrieved from https://www.drugabuse.gov/publications/drugfacts/comorbidity-addiction-other-mental-disorders

Looking at the statistics from chapter 0—65 percent of high school seniors engaged in sexual intercourse, 93 percent of boys and 62 percent of girls are exposed to porn by age 18, etc.—I think it's safe to say, as a society, reality is hitting us pretty hard. I have read many books and heard many lectures where statistics are cited. Google and Facebook are demonized as evil marketers trading the souls of our youth for monetized apps and websites, and declarations of change are touted. Yet, for all of the education, passion for purity, and sheer terror of the latest disturbing stats, the problem seems to only get worse. Why? Especially within a community of believers?

So far, every pornography study I have seen based on a church population is just as disturbing as the same study of a secular population. It would make sense if we didn't know the truth, but we do; that's kind of our thing—knowing and being set free by the truth. We know that we are made in God's image, that our sexuality is God's design, and that pornography is a perversion of that design. So why do we continue to find ourselves standing half-naked on the bathroom scale of life, morally obese?

## THE PROGRESSIVE PROCESS OF ADDICTION _

No one consciously decides to become an addict. It is a process that is progressive.[48] At the most basic level, we are looking for something or someone to change our mood, to change how we're feeling in the moment. The mechanism we choose can be almost anything. As mentioned previously, we are looking for that

---

[48] Nakken, C. (1996). *The Addictive Personality: Understanding the Addictive Process and Compulsive Behavior*. Center City, MN: Hazelden Publishing.

specific action, event, or relationship that is going to stimulate the production of dopamine in our brain, elevating our mood and making us feel better. Most often, we don't even know it's happening. For example, let's say you have a stressful day at work and decide to blow off steam and relax through Facebook. Keep in mind that although you have done this hundreds of times, what you're looking for is something that will change your mood and make you *feel* better. While online, you receive a friend request from an old high school relationship. In the moment, that friend request becomes the perfect "something" that makes you feel excited—the "something" that gives your brain a big hit of dopamine and relieves your stressful feelings. You immediately respond and begin messaging your old friend.

Over the next few months you invest in this online relationship, spending much more time on Facebook. Recently, your old friend wasn't available one evening. Feeling disappointed and a bit rejected, you sent out a few new friend requests of your own, sparking more new online relationships.

Although your company policy prohibits personal Facebook use during working hours, you have been caught and reprimanded for it while on the clock. This is not like you. You have always been a model employee and feel ashamed by your behavior; however, you tell yourself, "I am a better worker when I feel happy, even if I'm violating policy." In the moment, this minimizes your feelings of shame. Instead of hanging out with friends after work, which you used to do, you rush home to spend the evening online. Throughout your day, you ruminate over last night's conversations with all your new online friends, anticipating and fantasizing that tonight will be even better. You can't wait to get home! These new relationships are so captivating that even when feeling stressed, you have found a new way to cope. You have a sense of belonging that you haven't felt in a long time. This is your reality: Life feels great!

Now many of you might think, *There's really nothing wrong with this behavior, at least not at an "addicted" level, and who doesn't check Facebook at work?* To some extent, you're right. The behavior alone is not the problem. It becomes a problem when it is pervasive—when it becomes our "go-to" activity when feeling stressed, further disrupts our life, or causes us to become the worst version of ourselves. Additionally, at some point, whatever we are using to "feel better" is going to disappoint us or not be enough; and we are faced with having to increase our usage to get the same feeling or replace our "something" with something new.

We unknowingly create a catalyst by which our addictive behaviors flourish. In the above example, feeling stressed is the trigger, but finding a new online relationship is the fix. Although there were feelings of shame, rejection, and disappointment along the way, a pattern emerges: When I feel stressed, rejected or disappointed, finding new online relationships will make me feel better. Regardless of the mechanism we use—shopping, gambling, food, sex, alcohol, exercise, pornography, work, relationships, or the Internet—once we become addicted, it shapes and influences our perception of reality.

As Christian Internet users we are committed to reality only at the high cost of pornography. In the same way obesity was counter to who I believed I was, pornography is counter to who we claim to be as Christians. We say, "That's reality. I struggle with porn, or my kids struggle with porn. I didn't know it before, but I know it now; and darn it, I'm buckling down and fixing it!" The problem is that there are many unhealthy steps along the way where we fail to embrace reality at much lower costs.

In the same way I was not willing to accept the reality that I was using food and work to cope with the challenges of life, I believe there are many places online that we are not accepting reality. As users, we are not present and aware. We live in the fake reality (or fantasy) of the Internet. We believe that our online relationships have the same depth and built-in character as our in-person relationships. We spend more and more time "connecting" online only to find ourselves more and more isolated.

In the same way I so desperately wanted to be liked and respected by those around me, Internet users obsessively check feeds and updates or post on their timeline in hopes of a like or comment that will make them feel of value and worth. This repeated compulsive behavior can create a false sense of value that ironically moves them further and further from the vulnerability of a real relationship and further into isolation. There is a thrill of excitement when someone recognizes your value, but recognition without being known is empty. This emptiness will drive the user deeper into isolation, seeking out more destructive behaviors.

The problem is that, just like an addiction to food or work, an Internet or pornography addiction is a process addiction—a non-substance addiction.[49] A process addiction is often connected to a compulsive, destructive behavior. Unlike a substance addiction, you can't simply stop the behavior. Take for instance a food addiction (a process addiction) and compare it to a heroin addiction (a substance addiction). If you are a heroin addict, technically you can stop the behavior because you can stop using the drug. Physically, you do not need heroin to sustain life. On the

---

[49] Potenza, M. (2014). "Non-substance addictive behaviors in the context of DSM-5." Addict Behavior, 39(1).

other hand, if you are a food addict, you can't just stop eating. At some point, you will need to eat something to sustain life.

What makes a pornography addiction interesting is that it is not directly something we need to sustain life; however, pornography use is related to our sexuality. God created us as sexual beings. We can't stop being sexual beings any more than we can simply stop eating food. The key is to have healthy eating habits that nourish our body. In the case of our sexuality, we need to be healthy sexual beings.

## HEALTHY SEXUALITY _

Now you might be thinking, *I don't want my teenager to be a sexual being. I don't want them to engage in any sexual activity.* Believe me, I feel the same way about my kids. My point is that from birth you are a sexual being and identified as such. When you were born the doctor proudly declared, "It's a girl!" or "It's a boy!"

Healthy sexuality looks different at each stage of life. For grade schoolers, it's about age-appropriate education: Where do babies come from? Why did God make boys and girls different? How does my body work? What is pornography and why is it harmful for me? That last one is especially important, given that the average age a child first encounters pornography is 11 years old.[50]

For middle schoolers, sexual health is about puberty and learning to be comfortable with the changes going on in their body, as well as learning respectful, appropriate behavior with the opposite sex. High school is about stewardship—understanding the gift of sexuality God has given you and how to steward that

---

[50] Mueller, W. (2013). *A Parents' Primer on Internet Pornography. Center for Parent/Youth Understanding.* Retrieved from http://infoforfamilies.typepad.com/files/parent_primer_internet_pornography1.pdf

gift into marriage and beyond. Sexuality is much more than intercourse and reproduction. It's about understanding who God made you to be and that He has created (for most of us) the perfect spouse who will know us at a deeper level than any other human through the union of marriage. To quote my father, "True intimacy is not about being close and comfortable; it's about being uncomfortably close." This means that you know all of your spouse's faults and flaws, and you love them anyway.

It is important to understand the psychological and physiological changes happening in the brain and body of an adolescent as it pertains to their sexuality. When children begin to exhibit "teen behavior," most parents, and those who work closely with teens, attribute the behavior to hormonal activity.[51] However, when a two-year-old enters their "terrible twos," we don't attribute it to hormones; it's a reflection of the changes going on in their brain. The same is true of teenagers.

A child's brain will go through two phases of major brain construction: the first time when they are between the ages of three and five years old and the other beginning around twelve years old, spanning a good ten years, into their mid-twenties.

During the teen years, there are several forces at play, all of which impact a teen's brain and behavior. First of all, their brain is changing; it is pruning neurons that are no longer needed and myelinating the remaining neurons.[52] The same way an arborist would trim specific tree branches to strengthen the whole tree, the teen brain is pruning excess neurons in order to strengthen the overall function of the brain.

---

[51] Jensen, F. & Ellis Nutt, A. (2015). *The Teenage Brain: A Neuroscientist's Survival Guide to Raising Adolescents and Young Adults.* New York, NY: HarperCollins Publishers.

[52] Siegel, D. (2015). *Brainstorm: The Power and Purpose of the Teenage Brain.* New York, NY: Penguin Random House LLC.

Likewise, the myelination process—the development of a myelin sheath that insulates the axon of a neuron—strengthens neural connections, allowing information (electrical signals) to travel faster. Through this process, a teen's brain is undergoing a significant remodeling, transforming itself into an adult brain, involving different phases, at different times, and in different regions of the brain.

While these remarkable brain changes are happening under the surface, they will be evident through a teen's behavior. They will discover a new sense of awareness about themselves and others. As their brain changes, becoming more focused on complex concepts, so will their perception of the world around them. This will affect the way they think about and experience life. This will affect the way teens think about and respond to their friends, siblings, school, and parents. This is a healthy part of adolescence.

This major remodeling process isn't the only thing creating change in a teen's brain; it is also the time when teens—for the first time ever—experience a surge of sex hormones: testosterone, estrogen, and progesterone.[53] Not only is the teen brain accommodating the reconstruction that is taking place, but now, it's also adjusting to these never-before-experienced hormones.

As previously discussed, two essential brain areas are significantly impacted by these changes: the limbic system and the prefrontal cortex. Sex hormones are especially active in the limbic system, the emotional center of the brain. This contributes to the extreme fluctuation in the emotional response of teens, often experiencing severe mood swings. Since the prefrontal cortex is still developing—not fully developed until the mid-twenties—the teen brain is highly susceptible to sensation-

---

[53] Jensen, F. & Ellis Nutt, A. (2015). *The Teenage Brain: A Neuroscientist's Survival Guide to Raising Adolescents and Young Adults.* New York, NY: HarperCollins Publishers.

seeking. Because of this, teens lack the ability to make rational decisions and have limited impulse control.

So now, as if things were not challenging enough for teens, add to the mix the Internet: Anything, Anytime, Anywhere.

Although the teen years are an exciting time of emotional expression, sexual awareness, social connectedness, and novelty-seeking exploration, it can be a time of great turbulence. While the amazing changes happening in a teen's brain are necessary for adulthood, it is also what contributes to a teen's vulnerability when it comes to developing addictive behaviors. What happens during this season of change can have a profound and lasting effect on many patterns of behavior that are carried into adulthood.

In the next few chapters we will take a look at the more subtle steps that move Internet users from simply being targeted for marketing into isolation and, eventually, out of control pornography addicts. If we, as a society or as a community of Christ-followers, are paying attention to the more subtle cues and costs of Internet use, we can see lasting change in the pornography statistics, as well as the health and healing of families.

## 3  CHAPTER RECAP
## HIGHLIGHTS FROM "INTERNET ADDICTION—IT'S A PROCESS"

**Reality at All Costs.** Reality at all costs is not a mantra of extreme commitment or will power, but a state of mind; being present and aware. Reality at all costs is about knowing the truth and being willing to admit where my behavior does not match.

**We know the truth.** So far, every pornography study I have seen based on a church population is just as disturbing as the same study of a secular population. It would make sense if we didn't know the truth, but we do; that's kind of our thing—knowing and being set free by the truth. We know that we are made in God's image, that our sexuality is God's design, and that pornography is a perversion of that design.

**The Process of Addiction.** No one consciously decides to become an addict. It is a process that is progressive. At the most basic level, we are looking for something or someone to change our mood, to change how we're feeling in the moment. The mechanism we choose can be almost anything.

**A Vicious Cycle.** We unknowingly create a catalyst by which our addictive behaviors flourish. Regardless of the mechanism we use—shopping, gambling, food, sex, alcohol, exercise, pornography, work, relationships, or the Internet—once we become addicted, it shapes and influences our perception of reality.

**A Process Addiction?** The problem is that, just like an addiction to food or work, an Internet or pornography addiction is a process addiction—a non-substance addiction. A process addiction is often connected to a compulsive, destructive behavior. Unlike a substance addiction, you can't simply stop the behavior.

**Healthy Sexuality.** Healthy sexuality looks different at each stage of life.

**Sexuality and the Teen Brain.** It is important to understand the psychological and physiological changes happening in the brain and body of an adolescent as it pertains to their sexuality. During the teen years, there are several forces at play, all of which impact a teen's brain and behavior.

**Under Construction.** As a teen's brain changes, becoming more focused on complex concepts, so will their perception of the world around them. This will affect the way they think about and experience life.

**The Cost of Internet Use.** If we, as a society or as a community of Christ-followers, are paying attention to the more subtle cues and costs of Internet use, we can see lasting change in the pornography statistics, as well as the health and healing of families.

# I WANT TO BE A TRUST ENGINEER

About three years ago, my wife and I realized that we were spending most of our days in the downtown area of our fine city: Gresham, Oregon. Both the counseling and production offices for Pure Desire, as well as the performing arts studio where my wife works are in the downtown area. Our church is right in the middle of downtown and our gym is less than a mile away.

At the time, we were looking to relocate because the home we were renting was up for sale. As much as we liked our space (the house we were renting was set on ten acres), we thought, "Why not? Let's move downtown." It was sort of a reverse *Green Acres*. After renting a little 1950s cottage-style house for about eighteen months, we liked the neighborhood so much we bought the house, with the proviso that we would add a bathroom. It might be a First World problem, but when you have two kids and one bathroom, it's still a pretty big problem. One of my favorite things about living downtown is that our whole family walks everywhere; it's like a built-in exercise program. It's only a quarter mile to work, but there and back every day really adds up.

Shortly after moving into the house, while on my walk home from work, I saw a nondescript, gray building with a group of people huddled outside in a designated smoking area. I thought this was odd; most times, when I had walked by before, the building and parking lot were completely empty.

As I got closer I noticed that the people smoking weren't employees on break. They weren't relaxed and casually enjoying every slow, long drag. No, these people were nervously huffing and puffing—as if it was a chain-smoking contest. I noticed a man sitting in a folding chair off to the side of the group. I said, "Excuse me, sir, what is this building? Is there a meeting here tonight?" He pointed to a sign on the side of the building that had the letters ECAA printed on it and said, "It's an AA meeting."

Later, I found out that ECAA stands for East County Alcoholics Anonymous. I asked him, "Why is everyone smoking…vigorously?"

He smirked and chuckled a bit as he replied, "Yeah, they are a bit nervous. We don't allow smoking inside, so they are getting it out of their system while they can."

This piqued my curiosity. "What are they so nervous about?" I asked.

He turned my direction and folded his arms as if I had just asked the most ridiculous question possible. He replied, "They're all nervous to talk about not drinking for the next hour and a half."

For the rest of my walk home, I continued to think about my conversation with the man in the folding chair. The 12-step AA model was a very different process of addiction recovery than what I was walking through in my *Seven Pillars of Freedom* Pure Desire group. I thought about my own comorbidity, not only dealing with my addiction to food but also my addiction to work and how the two seemed to be inseparably intertwined.

I realized that the AA experience was much more about behavioral change than transformation, but the image of people smoking to cope with not drinking seemed so—I don't know how to describe it other than like "the old lady who swallowed a fly syndrome." You remember that book you read when you were a kid about an old lady who swallowed a fly, then a spider, a bird, a cat, a dog, a goat, a cow and finally a horse, which killed her, of course.

At some point in life, everyone has swallowed a fly, but no one in their right mind would even consider the barnyard binge the old lady went on that fateful day. I'll agree that spiders are known to eat flies, birds are known to eat spiders, but a cow and a horse? Those are both herbivores. What was the old lady thinking! And why were those people, who were so focused on not drinking, chain smoking?

## THE HIERARCHY OF ADDICTIONS _

I imagine that several attendees may have been court-ordered to attend the meeting as a result of a DUI, but I still couldn't wrap my brain around it. I realize that drunk driving causes death and destruction, not only for alcoholics but also innocent citizens. I understand how destructive an alcoholic can be within the family unit. My father had an alcoholic mom who made his childhood a living hell.

I also understand the devastation tobacco use can cause. My grandmother on my mom's side was a smoker all of her life, died of lung cancer, and most likely contributed to my grandfather's death. According to the CDC,[54] half a million people die from cigarette smoke each year in the United States alone, while only about 10,000 are killed in alcohol-impaired driving accidents.[55]

---

[54] National Center for Chronic Disease Prevention and Health Promotion, Office on Smoking and Health. Retrieved from https://www.cdc.gov/tobacco/data_statistics/fact_sheets/fast_facts/index.htm

[55] National Center for Chronic Disease Prevention and Health Promotion, National Center for Injury Prevention and Control, Division of Unintentional Injury Prevention. Retrieved from https://www.cdc.gov/motorvehiclesafety/impaired_driving/impaired-drv_factsheet.html

I state those two statistics not to compare which addiction is worse: smoking or drinking. Anyone who has lost a loved one as a result of addiction knows that it doesn't matter the drug, it's still incredibly senseless and painful. My point is, why do we as a society evaluate addictions? Why do we put them on a scale of heroin at the top—the worst of the worst—and food closer to the bottom—a socially acceptable addiction? If you were simply looking at the annual death toll, smoking is fifty times higher than drinking. Yet, for some reason, we deem the addiction to smoking as not only acceptable, but as a means to cope with fixing the addiction to drinking alcohol, which we arbitrarily see as much worse.

Since that day, I have given much thought to what constitutes a socially acceptable addiction. Clearly the AA meeting attendees knew the negative health effects of smoking. They had all read the Surgeon General's warning, but in that moment, in that community, somehow smoking was totally acceptable.

As I started to make changes in my own life—working less, exercising regularly, and developing a healthy diet—I begin to notice "the old lady who swallowed a fly syndrome" in my own circles and community. Before I walked by the ECAA hall, I never realized that workaholism and food addiction are not only accepted in my church, but celebrated. I'm not saying that my church has some whacked form of evangelical food and work-loving theology. I'm referring to how we all "do church." As part of my job, I visit dozens of churches every year, and my church is no exception. Think about the last church function or get-together you attended. Most likely, it was potluck style, with a variety of foods and probably not the healthiest foods. If there was a salad, it was likely the potato variety. If it was a barbecue, hot dogs or hamburgers were served and chips are often a popular side dish.

Food is a staple of church fellowship and functions. Every church leader knows if you need people to volunteer for something, bring food, especially doughnuts. Church people love a good potluck or picnic. Now, there is nothing wrong with the body of Christ eating together. Many times in the New Testament it was recorded that Jesus ate with His disciples and people He met in His ministry. Heck, He even ate at a tax collector's house.

The problem isn't the act of eating together, it's that we don't have the depth of relationship where we can be honest about our eating. No one ever says, "Wow, it is unbelievably difficult to stay on my diet and attend this church." I've lost count of the number of times, while on my way to serve at our children's center, I would tell myself: "Don't eat the doughnuts in the volunteer room. Don't eat the doughnuts in the volunteer room. Don't eat the doughnuts in the volunteer room!" Only to find myself eating a doughnut. Why? Everyone else was in the volunteer room eating doughnuts. Maybe I just wanted to fit in.

Then there's work. This one is a bit more subtle but it's there. So many times we as Christians equate work with providing for our family. This is especially true for men. You'll recall the most quoted scripture that isn't in the Bible: *God helps those who help themselves (Fallacations 10:3).*

More often than not, when I ask a friend at church, "How are you doing?" they respond with news about their job, a promotion, a home project, how their kids are doing in school or the six different sports they're involved with. Although my church doesn't preach it, for some reason as a community of believers we all take the perspective that God really values hard work: Jesus is coming soon...so look busy! We drive bigger, better cars and live in larger houses. We praise God for the promotions and seek wisdom when finances are tight. I'm not saying that managing a budget or talking to God about our finances is a bad thing; in fact, I think most Christians (myself included) could benefit from spending more time and energy doing both. My point is that somehow we seem prone to equate the quality of our relationship with Jesus with the size of our house, car, or bank account.

I didn't know it at the time, but when I decided to leave my high-tech job and become a nonprofit director, it was less about following God's call to ministry and more about God delivering me from a huge house, three cars, an RV, and a ton of other things I didn't know I could live without.

Our little downtown house has less than one third the square footage of our old house. We now have one car (and a little one at that—my kids call it the clown car) and no RV. My income is about half; and surprisingly, my wife, kids, and I are much happier with life than we were with all of our stuff. When money is tight, I have learned to change my perspective from thinking, *What's wrong with me? I'm not good enough; I should work harder,* to *Oh cool, God is about to do something big in our lives. Maybe there's something else I didn't know we could live without, or maybe He is going to provide for us in a unique and unusual way!* In case you're wondering, that last part is easier said than done. I still go to the "You're not good enough" response for a while before the "God wants the best for me" perspective kicks in. I'm getting better at it.

## THE GRAY AREAS OF ONLINE BEHAVIOR _

It is important to recognize the gray areas of online behavior that we tend to see as socially acceptable. Behaviors that we might see as benign as a box of doughnuts at a church function, are, all the while, still leading us down a road of separation from God. Now please, don't misunderstand what I'm saying; I'm not saying that working hard, cars, a big house, or doughnuts are evil. Well, maybe those Krispy Kreme Original Glazed. Seriously, have you tried one of those when the fresh sign is on? I've heard of drugs that cause dependency after the first hit, but I had no idea that a doughnut could do that!

Back to my point: we are created for dependency. The problem is when we put a job, a house, a car, or even a doughnut in the place of God, we stop trusting God and put our trust in things, others, or ourselves. We say, "I just need to try harder" or "If everyone else could get their act together" or "I just need this thing to feel better." Addiction, at its core, is a perversion of God's design for our dependence on Him. Over and over the Bible declares our dependence on and need for God:

*I am the bread of life. Your ancestors ate the manna in the wilderness, yet they died. But here is the bread that comes down from heaven, which anyone may eat and not die.*
JOHN 6:48-50

*But blessed is the one who trusts in the LORD, whose confidence is in him. They will be like a tree planted by the water that sends out its roots by the stream. It does not fear when heat comes; its leaves are always green. It has no worries in a year of drought and never fails to bear fruit.*
JEREMIAH 17:7-8

*I am the vine; you are the branches. If you remain in me and I in you, you will bear much fruit; apart from me you can do nothing.*
JOHN 15:5

Addiction takes hold when we attempt to replace our dependence on God with a dependence on something else. I remember reciting John 15:5 every morning just to get my head on straight. It is a sobering verse for the workaholic. Workaholics **hate** depending on anyone but themselves. Addiction always leads to isolation from God and others. Regardless of the addiction—work, food, drugs, sex, shopping, pornography, gambling, the Internet, and ironically, even love addicts (compulsively using relationships to feel loved)—we all end up in isolation.

Amazingly good things can happen when the Internet—Anything, Anytime, Anywhere—happens in community:

- Khan Academy: provides a free, world-class education for anyone, anywhere.

- Pure Desire counseling: 70 percent of our clients meet our counselors online because they live hundreds or thousands of miles away.

- Telehealth provides healthcare access in rural communities where there are no doctors.

These are just a few examples where the power of the Internet has been applied to community in a healthy way.

When Anything, Anytime, Anywhere happens in isolation it can be very destructive. The worst danger of the Internet is not pornography; it is isolation. I believe that isolation leads users to pornography, not the other way around. You could argue that when someone sees pornography they fall into a trap that the enemy has set to put them in isolation. While that is true to some degree, at some level, every porn addict I have ever met is using pornography to mask a wound they feel, one they cannot bring before the throne of God, and one they dare not expose to their friends, especially their church friends.

Johann Hari, author of *Chasing the Scream*, describes addiction and isolation this way:

## THE OPPOSITE OF ADDICTION IS NOT SOBRIETY. THE OPPOSITE OF ADDICTION IS CONNECTION.[56]

If isolation is the challenge for addicts and ultimately Gen Z Internet users, and connection is what they need to keep from developing an addiction to the Internet and pornography, as people with influence in their lives, where do we start?

## A SURPRISING EXPERIMENT _

A great place to glean insight is an inadvertent, yet telling, behavioral study conducted by Facebook. First, to give some perspective on the scale and size of the Facebook community: if the total number of Facebook users represented a country, it would be the largest population in the world (bigger than China).[57] So when I say behavioral study, I'm not just talking about a case study of 100 users. I am talking about one in seven people in the world with a Facebook account.

As Facebook grew to a size never before seen by a social network service, some pretty bizarre things started happening. It started near the end of 2011, between the week of Christmas and New Year's

---

[56] Hari, J (2015). *Chasing the Scream: The First and Last Days of the War on Drugs*. New York, NY: Bloomsbury USA.

[57] Matthew, J. (2015). "Facebook is now more 'populous' than China with 1.44 billion monthly active users." International Business Times. April 23. Retrieved from http://www.ibtimes.co.uk/facebook-now-more-populous-china-1-44-billion-monthly-active-users-1497909

Day.[58] In that one week, Facebook users uploaded more photos than all of the photos stored on Flickr (a leading online photo storage service), ever. As happy as the executives at Facebook were to see the popularity of their service explode, the engineers were not so happy. Along with the millions of uploaded photos were millions of reports. Most large service providers, like Facebook, rely on their users to report content that violates their policies: posts and pictures of criminal activity, hate speech, drug use, and nudity, among others. Looking at the sheer volume of reports from users that the engineers were tasked with resolving, they decided to do some investigating to see what they were up against.

Looking at the data, they found that 97 percent of the reports were inaccurate; a picture of a family in Christmas sweaters reported as nudity, a picture of a mom holding a baby reported as harassment, a photo of a puppy reported as hate speech. Completely bewildered, the engineers decided to contact the users who filed the report and simply ask, "Why don't you like this photo?" The answers astonished the engineers. In almost every report, they found that the person making the complaint was in the photo. Additionally, they discovered that there was some form of relational tension at play between the person who posted the photo and the person complaining about the photo. Many of the photos included an ex: girlfriend, boyfriend, or spouse. The picture of the puppy labeled "hate speech" was the pet of a couple who had ended their relationship. The mom with the baby thought the photo was unflattering.

At this point, the engineers found themselves in a bit of a pickle. They couldn't take the photos down simply because a

---

[58] Radiolab Podcast Articles (2015). "The Trust Engineers." February 9. Retrieved from http://www.radiolab.org/story/trust-engineers/

user reported, "I don't like this friend," or "They posted an ugly picture of me." Facebook had no policy to deal with a photo that someone simply didn't like. The obvious solution to the problem would be to tell the user filing the complaint to contact their friend who posted the photo and ask to have it removed. As a service provider funded by advertisements, they didn't want to risk alienating users. Without a clear way to handle the problem, they decided to do an experiment. The plan was to:

1. contact the users who wanted the photo removed in order to understand their point of view,

2. help them formulate a request to remove the photo, and

3. send it to their friend who posted the photo.

Their goal was to persuade the users filing the complaint to contact the user who posted the photo to settle the conflict. In essence, they were attempting to engineer conflict resolution. They also decided to unofficially retitle themselves as "Trust Engineers" because their goal was to engineer mechanisms that build trust with the user filing the complaint. Each Friday afternoon the Trust Engineers would meet with scientists and psychologists from local universities to review the data from their interactions with users.

They started by asking users, "How does this picture make you feel?" They gave the users several emotional choices to describe how the picture made them feel; some of the choices included embarrassing, upsetting, saddening, and bad picture. They also included an "other" box for users to fill in their own response. As the responses came in, they found that 50 percent of users filing complaints selected one of the choices provided and approximately 34 percent picked "other." In reviewing the "other" responses, the engineers were astonished to find that the vast majority of respondents wrote "it's embarrassing."

The engineers were completely perplexed: "embarrassing" was one of the choices provided on the list of responses. Nevertheless, on the list of multiple-choice responses, they decided to change "embarrassing" to "it's embarrassing." Sure enough, when the new set of responses came in with "it's embarrassing" as one of the choices, the number of users selecting an emotion increased from 50 percent to 78 percent. In Facebook metrics this is no anomaly. A 28 percent increase represents thousands of respondents. After seeing this dramatic shift in responses, simply by adding the word "it's," they came to a new realization: without the additional word, users made the assumption that the original "embarrassing" selection implied that the user was embarrassed, whereas "it's" made it clear that the photo was embarrassing.

Now the tricky part: knowing how the users felt about these photos, how could they help them move those feelings into a removal request to the user who posted the photo? They started by adding a simple text box that appeared after users identified how they felt. It read, "We think it's a good idea to tell your friend that they upset you."

In this first iteration with the empty text box, only about 20 percent of users completed the form to send. The engineers decided to try the message box again, but this time, they populated it with a suggested message to get the ball rolling. Immediately, they saw the number of messages sent jump from 20 percent to 50 percent. With 50 percent of the complaints now solving themselves—that ultimately the engineers couldn't resolve— the engineers saw a light at the end of the tunnel. They tried a variety of different suggested messages, such as "I'm so sorry to bother you, but I don't like this photo. Would you please take it down?" or "Hey, I don't like this photo. Take it down." It turns out that the two most effective messages were:

- *Hey, I don't like this photo. Take it down.*
- *Hey, I don't like this photo. Would you please take it down?*

If isolation is the challenge for Gen Z Internet users, and connection is what they need to keep from developing an addiction, what are the takeaways from the Facebook experiment? This experiment is empirical verification of what researchers have been saying for a number of years. In an article regarding the effects of screen time and brain function, Dr. Victoria L. Dunckley, author and child psychiatrist, summarizes the negative effects of excessive screen time has on the brain:

*A finding of particular concern was damage to an area known is the insula, which is involved in our capacity to develop **empathy** and compassion for others and our ability to integrate physical signals with emotion. Aside from the obvious link to violent behavior, these skills dictate the depth and quality of **personal relationships**.*[59]

In the Facebook experiment we see these same elements:

- A lack of empathy: users were not able to take on their friend's perspective regarding why they posted the photo and preferred a direct message without the appearance of an apology.

- Poor personal relationship skills: users wanted to avoid writing their own response and expected Facebook to solve their problem.

---

[59] Dunckley, V. (2014). "Gray Matters: Too Much Screen Time Damages the Brain: Neuroimaging research show excessive screen time damages the brain." Psychology Today. February 27. Retrieved from https://www.psychologytoday.com/blog/mental-wealth/201402/gray-matters-too-much-screen-time-damages-the-brain

There are many online organizations with virtually limitless resources that are attempting to engineer relationships for this simple reason: more users equals a greater opportunity to advertise to those users. Facebook may have been the first, but now they are only one of many organizations that employ social engineering techniques to gain and retain users.

## EMPATHY AND THE INTERNET _

Looking at what we have learned about the nature of the Internet—producing a self-focused impulsive generation, lacking in empathy, with poor relational skills—all of a sudden, the pornography statistics make more sense. How can a good kid, who loves Jesus with all their heart, get tangled up in a pornography addiction? Simple: they may love Jesus, they may go to church every week, and maybe they are even part of the worship team at youth group; but everyone has wounds and everyone gets hurt. When you combine woundedness and a lack of empathy with self-centeredness, poor relational skills, and impulsivity, the statistics begin to make a lot more sense.

Although content filters and accountability programs are part of the solution, it needs to begin with cultivating empathy through face-to-face relationships. To empathize with someone is not only understanding what they may be feeling, but taking on what they are feeling as though you were in their situation.[60] It requires a level of emotional awareness that we are not born with; empathy is a learned behavior. Many children begin to develop empathy at a young age. When a child sees a sibling crying, they

---

60  Kutner, L. (2016). "How Children Develop Empathy." Psych Central. Retrieved on from https://psychcentral.com/lib/how-children-develop-empathy/

may offer the sibling a toy or some form of comfort. They may not be able to identify what their sibling is feeling other than they're sad and perhaps a toy will make them feel better.

Technology has become such an essential part of human communication, decreasing the amount of time spent in face-to-face communication.[61] One study conducted by the Kaiser Family Foundation found that young people, ages 8 to 18, spend more time on various forms of media—an average of 7.5 hours per day—than any other activity. Research suggests that people who engage in face-to-face conversations report higher levels of empathy than those who converse using technology.

Think about this: when we have an in-person conversation, we are acutely aware of another's attitudes and feelings, based on their body language, as well as their verbal and nonverbal cues; they use voice inflection and gestures. There is a natural give-and-take in the conversation, developed through eye contact and expression, cultivating the essence of reciprocal interaction: each person both impacting and impacted by the other person.[62] Face-to-face communication facilitates an important socialization skill and is instrumental in developing empathy.

Let's say you're having lunch with a friend and you say something that hurts their feelings. How do you know? You can see their face; you can easily read their expression and body language. In that moment, you feel bad. It was not your intent to hurt their feelings, so you quickly apologize and explain what you meant. You instantly work to repair and restore the relationship.

---

[61] Drago, E. (2015). "The Effect of Technology on Face-to-Face Communication." The Elon Journal of Undergraduate Research in Communications, 6(1). Spring.

[62] Lehan, T. (2017). "Reciprocal Interaction: Definition & Model." Retrieved from http://study.com/academy/lesson/reciprocal-interaction-definition-model-quiz.html#transcriptHeader

Digital communication has disrupted this developmental piece for Generation Z. Here's why: When communicating digitally, you cannot see the other person. You cannot read their facial expressions. You cannot hear the tone of their words or visually interpret their nonverbal cues. You can say something hurtful, unintentionally of course, but may never know how it made them feel. In many ways, digital communication has eliminated reciprocal interaction, minimizing how we develop empathy and build relationships. In fact, it has been suggested that the lack of time young people spend interacting face-to-face may have "significant consequences on their development of social skills" and strongly influence their sense of self.[63]

I titled this chapter "I Want to Be a Trust Engineer" because I love the philosophy behind what the Facebook engineers were trying to do: their goal was to engineer mechanisms that build trust with the user. What if that was one of our core goals? What if we were intentional about "building trust" with our kids and with the young people we influence? Not through digital communication, but through intentional face-to-face communication. I think this would have a tremendous impact on the next generation and is an area where I plan to invest with my own kids and others with whom I have influence. I would encourage you to do the same so that collectively we can continue to positively influence the next generation.

A smile or hug emoji just isn't the same as the real thing.

---

[63] Drago, E. (2015). "The Effect of Technology on Face-to-Face Communication." The Elon Journal of Undergraduate Research in Communications, 6(1). Spring.

## CHAPTER RECAP
# HIGHLIGHTS FROM "I WANT TO BE A TRUST ENGINEER"

(4)

**The Hierarchy of Addictions.** Anyone who has lost a loved one as a result of addiction knows that it doesn't matter the drug, it's still incredibly senseless and painful. Why do we as a society evaluate addictions? Why do we put them on a scale of heroin at the top (the worst of the worst) and food closer to the bottom because it is a socially acceptable addiction?

**Workaholism.** For some reason, as a community of believers we all take the perspective that God really values hard work: Jesus is coming soon...so look busy!

**The Gray Areas of Online Behavior.** It is important to recognize the gray areas of online behavior that we tend to see as socially acceptable. Behaviors that we might see as benign are, all the while, still leading us down a road of separation from God.

**We Were Designed for Dependency.** Addiction takes hold when we attempt to replace our dependence on God with a dependence on something else.

**Addiction and Isolation.** Addiction always leads to isolation from God and others. Regardless of the addiction—work, food, drugs, sex, shopping, pornography, gambling, the Internet, and ironically, even love addicts (compulsively using relationships to feel loved)—we all end up in isolation.

**The Worst Danger of the Internet?** When Anything, Anytime, Anywhere happens in isolation it can be very destructive. The worst danger of the Internet is not pornography; it is isolation.

**Facebook Cares.** There are many online organizations with virtually limitless resources that are attempting to engineer relationships for this simple reason: more users equals a greater opportunity to advertise to those users. Facebook may have been the first, but now they are only one of many organizations that employ social engineering techniques to gain and retain users.

**What is Empathy?** To empathize with someone is not only understanding what they may be feeling, but also taking on what they are feeling as though you were in their situation.

**A Lack of Empathy.** When you combine woundedness and a lack of empathy with self-centeredness, poor relational skills, and impulsivity, the pornography statistics begin to make a lot more sense.

**Empathy is a Learned Behavior.** Technology has become such an essential part of human communication, decreasing the amount of time spent in face-to-face communication. Face-to-face communication facilitates an important socialization skill and is instrumental in developing empathy.

**Becoming a Trust Engineer.** What if we were intentional about "building trust" with our kids and with the young people we influence? Not through digital communication, but through intentional face-to-face communication. This would have a tremendous impact on the next generation.

# | BINARY AND EMPATHY

I've always wondered what it would be like to have a normal job—maybe as a salesperson, a software programmer, or an electrician. So far, my career after college has consisted of a laser engineer in the aerospace industry and operations director of a nonprofit parachurch ministry whose main focus is sexual addiction recovery. In both cases, as you can imagine, I've run into some very unique people.

At Pure Desire, I often find myself sharing the events of my weekend with a coworker, followed by them asking, "How did that make you feel?" or I receive an accountability notification regarding one of the counselors, who downloaded a research paper about functional MRI's of subjects who are acting out sexually in uh…let's just say, very unusual ways.

As a laser engineer, I ran into even more unique people! I recall (more than once) having to intervene in a heated argument between two engineers about the most efficient way to calculate pi. There was also the time I had to talk to HR because someone had filed a complaint arguing that Klingon was in fact a foreign language and therefore protected by the Oregon Department of Employment's anti-language discrimination policy; ergo, he should be able to speak Klingon at work without being harassed by coworkers. There was the challenge every summer when multiple employees would request the same week off to attend Comic-Con. I distinctly remember asking one of the engineers why he had *The Lord of the Rings*[64] theme song as his ringtone and he replied, "It is the ring that rules them all!"

Even though I've worked with many, I don't really consider myself a nerd (my family would probably argue that point). There are, however, a few things that might push me into the nerdy category. I'm not a Marvel movie fan, and I don't speak a word of Klingon; but, my favorite movie (and book series) is *The Hitchhiker's Guide to the Galaxy.*[65] It's hard to say why that movie is at the top of my list. I don't know if it's the over-the-top science fiction or the relentless satirical commentary about government, religion, and the human condition; or maybe it's just the opening number with all of the dolphins fleeing the Earth's imminent demise, while singing that catchy tune—"So Long, and Thanks for All the Fish!"

While doing research for this book, I was reminded of the character, Marvin; the chronically depressed robot.[66] Originally built as one of many failed prototypes of Sirius Cybernetics Corporation, Marvin was equipped with GPP (Genuine People Personalities) technology. Unlike stereotypical movie robots, Marvin had emotions, hopes, dreams, intelligence, and worst of all, the capacity for boredom (not a good trait for machines that are designed for repetitive tasks). Through the character of Marvin and other robots developed by Sirius Cybernetics Corporation, author Douglas Adams makes a satirical, yet

---

[64] Jackson, P. (2001). *The Lord of the Rings: The Fellowship of the Ring*. USA: New Line Cinema.

[65] Jennings, G. (2005). *The Hitchhiker's Guide to the Galaxy*. USA: Buena Vista Pictures.

[66] "Marvin." (2017). In Wikipedia, the Free Encyclopedia. Retrieved from https://en.wikipedia.org/w/index.php?title=Marvin&oldid=792928984

compelling, commentary about our unique ability as humans to feel emotions and experience empathy, and how ridiculous a task it would be to design a robot capable of these human attributes.

## BLACK-AND-WHITE THINKING _

Robots and computers use binary logic—a numeric system that only uses two digits: 0 and 1.[67] In fact, the word binary simply means "something having two parts." Streams of code and data move between zeros and ones to give direction to a computer's hardware. The binary system is the foundation on which digital technology is built.[68]

For humans, there are some benefits to binary thinking—otherwise known as black-and-white thinking. Good or bad, right or wrong, yes or no, happy or sad—these are all very simple.[69] Binary thinking feels safe. It allows us to maintain order and control in a chaotic world. It allows a person to only consider two potential answers or outcomes. It allows us to make split-second decisions, such as choosing between flight or fight when we sense danger. There is often no in-between. Unfortunately, this type of thinking also blinds us to the endless possibilities available outside the binary system, outside the realm of black and white.[70] Many

[67] Christensson, P. (2013, April 10). "Binary Definition." Retrieved from https://techterms.com

[68] "Binary system." BusinessDictionary.com. Retrieved from BusinessDictionary.com website: http://www.businessdictionary.com/definition/binary-system.html

[69] Priestley, D. (2015). "Binary Thinking vs Directional Thinking." Dent. Retrieved from file:///home/chronos/u-29837278fe21ac3eda5dd846cc0fafdd15b6d4c7/Downloads/Binary%20Thinking%20vs%20Directional%20Thinking%20-%20Key%20Person%20of%20Influence.mhtml

[70] Long, R. (2015). "The Good, Bad, and Ugly of Binary Thinking." The Center for Internet and Society. Retrieved from http://cyberlaw.stanford.edu/

people who use binary thinking get stuck in their black-and-white thinking, limited by their perceived choices, not aware of their available choices.

Black-and-white thinking deals with absolutes—an all-or-nothing thought process. This type of thinking is commonly found among individuals who struggle with addictive behaviors and often leads to emotionally charged decision-making.[71] When we live life under the constraints of binary thinking, we unknowingly put tremendous stress on our interpersonal relationships. We view our relationships as all-or-nothing: they either love me completely or not at all. This puts our relationships at risk due to the extreme expectations we put on others, demanding their undying love and loyalty without question.

Binary or black-and-white thinking creates conflict in our lives. Whether we realize it or not, this thought pattern interferes with our ability to rationalize our world. During a disagreement, the focus becomes more about proving someone wrong than about finding a resolution. It fuels a cognitive distortion in our thinking, suggesting that the opposing party is intentionally trying to hurt us and is therefore the enemy.

What makes matters worse is that it doesn't stop there. Black-and-white thinking often leads to negative thinking, minimizing or disregarding the positive things that happen in life and focusing on the negative things. For example: regardless of the fact that a person has maintained sobriety for five years, once they relapse, the focus is entirely on the relapse, not on the extended period of sobriety.

---

[71] The Ranch, (2012). "The Powerful Role of Cognitive Thinking Errors in Addiction." Retrieved from https://www.recoveryranch.com/articles/addiction-research/drug-addiction-drug-rehab-treatment/

Binary thinkers also have a tendency to overgeneralize a situation. Let's say Joe decides to join a recovery group. While most of the group members are very nice, when one person says something hurtful to Joe, he immediately leaves the group meeting, never to return, and believes wholeheartedly that all recovery groups are evil. This behavior leads to blaming. Blaming often plays a huge role in addictive behavior. Continuing with our recovery group scenario, since all recovery groups are evil, Joe can't attend *any* recovery group. Joe really wants to, but he can't bring himself to be among heartless individuals and risk feeling hurt. Joe thinks, quite frankly, that it is the fault of the recovery group members that he will never find healing from his addiction.

When we use binary or black-and-white thinking, we do not allow for open-minded learning and growth.[72] We don't allow for the many shades of gray in our world. Stepping outside of our black-and-white thinking box can be scary, but also very liberating. By doing so, you will experience the vast colors of our world through creative and innovative thought. As addicts, we might think that black-and-white thinking keeps us safe, but really, it puts a choke hold on our sobriety; it is what keeps us in bondage.

Humans were not designed to operate like a computer program, using only a binary process. We were designed to live in the gray, to experience the imperfections of life that provide an opportunity for us to change and undergo transformation. Once we break out of our black-and-white thinking, it allows us to apply the "gray grace" to others, lowering our expectations and cultivating authentic relationships.

---

[72] Mckibben, J. (2014). "The Dangers of Black and White Thinking." Palm Partners Recovery Center. Retrieved from http://blog.palmpartners.com/dangers-black-white-thinking/

## SHAME AND DISCONNECTION _

With the advancement of technology, it has become more challenging for all of us to intentionally develop face-to-face relationships, especially the parent-child relationship. Don't get me wrong; I know these advancements definitely have their advantages. Military families around the world see their loved ones through online connections via FaceTime and Skype, a privilege unknown to previous generations who relied on the postal service to maintain a connection with their loved ones. This is just one of many examples where technology is the hero.

For many of us, it is the daily use of technology that erodes the face-to-face connection we have with family and friends, leading to an unforeseen disconnection. A couple years ago, while having dinner at a friend's house, I was surprised to see my friend text their children to tell them dinner was ready. You may be thinking that the children were playing outside or at a neighbor's house, but they were downstairs playing Xbox. In that moment, I promised myself that I would never be that parent, that I would never let the convenience of my cell phone dictate the daily interactions I had with my kids. Of course, you know what they say about making promises you can't keep—it wasn't long before I became that parent, texting my kids about their chores, homework, and dinnertime while they were in the same house, only a few rooms away.

What's worse is that convenience becomes the culprit or the excuse used by many of us to maintain a more consistent relationship with our cell phone than with family and friends under the guise of staying connected. Using our cell phones to access the Internet, for socialization, work, or play—Anything,

Anytime, Anywhere—has become a cultural, if not, global epidemic. The statistics are staggering:[73]

- Over 1.8 billion people own a smartphone and use it on a daily basis.

- The average person checks their screen 150 times per day.

- Almost 70 percent of 11- to 12-year-olds use a mobile phone.

- Close to 90 percent of 14-year-olds use a mobile phone.

- Approximately 56 percent of children between the ages of 10 and 13 own a smartphone.

- It is estimated that 25 percent of children between ages 2 and 5 have a smartphone.

While many researchers are concerned with how cell phone use affects childhood brain development, which is a valid concern, others are equally concerned with how cell phone use contributes to a lack of interaction between parents and children.

During the early years of life, the interaction between parents and children is mainly positive, loving, and playful.[74] An infant's limited communication, mobility, and skills keep them reliant on their parents to meet their physical and emotional needs. However, as they grow into toddlers and become more vocal, mobile, and adaptive, they experience changes in their relationship with their parents. As a result of the child's newfound independence and curiosity, they are more at risk to the dangers of their environment. In an effort to protect their children parents become hypervigilant;

---

[73] Williams, A. (2016). "How Do Smartphones Affect Childhood Psychology?" Psych Central. Retrieved from https://psychcentral.com/lib/how-do-smartphones-affect-childhood-psychology/

[74] Cozolino, L. (2014). *The Neuroscience of Human Relationships: Attachment and the Developing Social Brain* (2nd ed.). New York, NY: W. W. Norton & Company, Inc.

the softly spoken words of affection are replaced with "No," "Stop," and "Don't touch that!" This is how shame develops on a subconscious level. Although these are words we have to say to our children, it is important that we are intentional in how we communicate both positive and negative words.

There is a type of shame that develops through our conscious interaction with others, improving our self-awareness, deepening our empathetic response and reinforcing our self-esteem. This is something we learn over time that keeps our behaviors in check. However, there is another type of shame that is developed on an unconscious level and is the product of consistent negative attachment experiences, producing an emotional perspective not based on a person's behavior, but based on their perception of themselves. Those who experience this deep level of shame carry the fundamental belief that they are defective, unlovable, and worthless. For a child who experiences shame in this way, they may come to believe that they are not an important member of the family, or that they are less valuable than the other family members.

Between 5 and 10 years of age, as we achieve self-awareness, shame and self-esteem are programmed into our social and emotional foundation. Dr. Louis Cozolino suggests,

IT IS SIMILAR IN MANY WAYS TO BOOTING UP YOUR COMPUTER AND BEING PRESENTED WITH A DESKTOP THAT HAS BEEN ORGANIZED BY A MICROSOFT OR APPLE OPERATING SYSTEM. YOU ACCEPT IT AS THE PARAMETERS OF YOUR COMPUTING UNIVERSE—UNAWARE OF THE THOUSANDS OF LINES OF PROGRAMMING LANGUAGE REQUIRED TO GENERATE THE REALITY THAT HAS BEEN CREATED FOR YOU.[75]

---

[75] Ibid. 285.

Simply put, shame and self-esteem become part of our programming at such an early age that most of us are unaware of how they affect our relationships and everyday lives.

Shame plays a significant role in a person's social life, whether they realize it or not; however, if you look closely, you may recognize the behaviors. It has a way of distorting the perception of social interactions, making a benign situation appear negative. Continual misinterpretation of social situations—perceived as dismissive or rejection—creates a vicious cycle that negatively affects their ability to form relationships.

At a foundational level, you can see how shame enters our world, potentially interfering with the development of healthy socialization skills. This includes our Internet behaviors. A recent study was conducted to investigate the correlation between social network usage, shame, and Internet addiction.[76] The results indicate that shame significantly and positively predicts social network usage and Internet addiction. While insecurity, low self-esteem, and social anxiety often coexist with shame, it is suggested that individuals who struggle with shame, are more likely to invest in online social networking as a means to cultivate relationships, rather than face-to-face relationships. It gives the individual a sense of connection while staying very disconnected. This study also revealed that greater social networking is associated with greater feelings of shame, creating a vicious cycle. For many individuals, shame is the root of disconnection.

---

[76] Dogan, U. & Kaya, S. (2016). "Mediation Effects of Internet Addiction on Shame and Social Networking." Universal Journal of Educational Research 4(5), 1037–1042.

# THE UNWORTHY ROOT _

The bigger issue lies in the fact that shame doesn't exist in a single, isolated, nicely wrapped definition. It often exists as the catalyst to an overabundance of feelings that many believe shape and define their identity. Shame is more than feeling badly about ourselves; it's feeling that we are bad.[77]

Feeling shame is personal. It creates a sense of incompetence and powerlessness; we feel helpless. For some, feeling a sense of shame may include feeling embarrassed, inadequate, or humiliated. Again, not because of something we did, but because of who we are on the inside. For others, feelings of self-condemnation and disdain rule their mind, keeping them trapped in an endless cycle of emotional punishment.

As we ruminate over our imperfections and shortcomings, our feeling of shame distracts us from seeing ourselves objectively. At our core, we believe that we are unworthy, that we are worthless. We've convinced ourselves that if others really knew us, they wouldn't like us. They wouldn't love us. One young man put it this way: "My shame makes it impossible for me to be loved because I can never believe someone could love me. And if I believe they do, I can't possibly respect them because if they love me, their judgment must be seriously flawed."[78]

In many ways, our feelings of worthlessness intensify our feelings of shame, telling us that we are of no value, that we have no good qualities and that we are deserving of contempt. Today, for many people—and not just the younger generations—their

---

[77] Beaumont, L. (2015). "Shame: We feel badly about ourselves." Retrieved from http://emotionalcompetency.com/shame.htm

[78] Cozolino, L. (2014). *The Neuroscience of Human Relationships: Attachment and the Developing Social Brain* (2nd ed.). New York, NY: W. W. Norton & Company, Inc.

feeling of value comes from social media. Their lives are lived in the public domain, affected by every selfie, tweet, tag, follower, friend, snapchat, retweet, and more.

In a recent study, researchers found that the use of social media puts tremendous pressure on its users as they attempt to create a personal brand of themselves, seeking to gain a sense of reassurance and acceptance through "likes and shares."[79] In a very real sense, they are using a virtual reality to create their identity, the identity that will make them feel valued and loved by others. Unfortunately, this pursuit of a false identity only leads to greater feelings of worthlessness and shame.

## CREATING A SENSE OF VALUE

As previously discussed, we develop our sense of self-worth—our value—at a very young age. This is learned through face-to-face communication and reciprocal interaction, primarily from a parent-child relationship. Through collaborative communication, both verbal and nonverbal, our thoughts, feelings, and actions receive validation, reinforcing our sense of self.[80] As a child communicates with a parent or caregiver, they interpret the reciprocal behaviors, facial expressions, and language. It is through this serve-and-return social construct that children develop a perception of who they are; they develop their identity.

This important aspect of childhood development and socialization cannot happen in isolation—it can only be created

---

[79] Owen, J. (2016). "Facebook and Twitter leaving millions of Britons depressed, study finds." The Independent Online. Retrieved from http://www.independent.co.uk/news/uk/home-news/facebook-twitter-depressed-uk-britain-millions-social-media-study-research-a6971686.html

[80] Siegel, D. & Hartzell, M. (2004). *Parenting from the Inside Out*. New York, NY: Tarcher Perigee.

through connection. No parent is perfect; however, when a child experiences positive connection with their parent, with greater frequency than negative connections, it bolsters their sense of self. On a daily basis, instead of listening and empathetically responding to our child's experience, we process their experience and feelings through our "parent" filter, failing to understand their dilemma and unsuccessfully making a connection.

It is imperative that parents learn to listen and understand their child's experiences in order for children to create a healthy sense of value. This is not an easy task for many parents because we tend to parent the way we were parented. We do not take the time to sit with our child in the midst of their despair—real or perceived—and help them make sense of their feelings. Let's say your daughter comes home from school and is obviously upset. She tells you how a boy made fun of her in front of the whole class. She tried not to cry and ran out of the class. How do you respond? Here's what most parents would say, "What did he say? (child answers) That doesn't seem like such a big deal. Definitely not worth crying over. Why do you care what a stupid boy says anyway?" As parents, we often err on the side of making matters worse and have to follow up with damage control.

Allowing your child to feel what they're feeling and experience the situation from a child's perspective is so valuable. I'll never forget watching my sister-in-law discipline my nephew and the way she dealt with the fallout. My nephew had engaged in a string of bad behaviors and received the punishment of no Xbox for two weeks. He immediately started crying and wanted to negotiate the punishment.

After a short communication exchange, my sister-in-law asked my nephew why he was so upset. He said, "I'm really, really sad and I want to cry, but you only want to talk."

My sister-in-law paused for a minute and then said, "Okay. I'm sorry you're sad. Why don't you take five minutes in your room to feel sad and then we'll finish talking about your punishment." It was amazing! After the five minutes had passed, my nephew came out of his room and was no longer upset; he was ready to have a conversation about the consequences of his actions.

If we were raised in an environment where we learned that emotional expression was not tolerated, then we may feel the same way with our own children. We have to be intentional about expressing our own emotions in a healthy way so that our children learn that feelings and emotional response are normal and part of God's design. As parents, we need to be emotionally vulnerable and let our children see us experience joy, love, excitement, sadness, pain, and disappointment. Our children learn empathy—the ability to identify with what another is thinking or feeling, and provide an appropriate emotional response—by observing and responding to our emotional experiences.[81] This emotional interaction reinforces their sense of connection and promotes their development of self. In many ways, a child's sense of self and value is rooted in connection.

## THIS IS WHO I AM _

You may be asking yourself, *What does all of this have to do with positively influencing the next generation, and how is this going to help me protect my kids from pornography?* Those are great questions. I hope you're beginning to see the connection between all of these factors—black-and-white thinking, shame, isolation,

---

[81] Ferrari, V., Smeraldi, E., Bottero, G. & Politi, E. (2014). "Addiction and empathy: a preliminary analysis." Neurological Sciences, 35, 855–859.

worthlessness, self-awareness, value, and empathy—and how they contribute to our identity.

When it comes to social media, young people are faced with amazing pressure—the pressure to be someone they're not. They find themselves in a constant state of comparison, wondering if their online profiles, photos, and connections measure up to the next guy. At some point, their profile no longer represents who they are on the inside, but represents who they think they have to be for their online friends and followers. Dr. Donna Wick, a clinical and developmental psychologist, suggests that, "Adolescence and the early twenties in particular are the years in which you are acutely aware of the contrasts between who you appear to be and who you think you are."[82] When it comes to social media use, one of the greatest challenges facing young people is letting go of who they "think they should be" and focusing on who they really are.

There is a strong correlation between developing empathy and a healthy sense of self. Empathy is what allows us to build connection with others, through mutual trust and understanding.[83] Think of empathy this way: it is the bridge that connects us to all the other significant relationships in our lives. When we experience some form of stress or hardship resulting in an emotional response, and our emotional response is mirrored back to us through an empathetic action, it reinforces our sense of self and value.

Let me give you an example. You pick up your teenage daughter from a school function and she is crying. You ask her,

[82] Ehmke, R. (2017). "How Using Social Media Affects Teenagers." Child Mind Institute, Inc. Retrieved from https://childmind.org/article/how-using-social-media-affects-teenagers/

[83] Catapano, J. (2017). "Teaching Strategies: The Importance of Empathy." Retrieved from http://www.teachhub.com/teaching-strategies-importance-empathy

"What's wrong?" and she says, "Nothing!" How do you respond? Do you harshly respond, "Well if nothing's wrong, then stop crying!"? Or do you pause, face your child who is hurting, and with an expression of love and an empathetic tone reply, "I'm so sorry you're upset. I would really like to help. Let me know if you want to talk about it." That's it; nothing more. Don't push; don't prod. Wait. Later that evening or the next day, when your daughter is ready to talk about it, just listen. Don't try and fix it. Just listen. Remember to validate her feelings; even if the reason she's upset seems trivial to you, it is important to her. Reinforcing the fact that she is entitled to her feelings reinforces her sense of self and value. It strengthens her feelings of worth and contributes to the development of her identity.

Research suggests that developing empathy improves interpersonal relationships, cultivating an environment of mutual respect and acceptance.[84] Empathy has been shown to reduce negative and aggressive behaviors, creating a relational atmosphere of healthy communication and harmony. It is a crucial element in creating healthy relationships, and like any other learned behavior, it has to be intentionally practiced so it becomes a natural part of our daily lives.

God did not design us to function in a binary world; He designed us for relationship, with Him and with others. As a foundational element of relationship, understanding the significance of empathy is key, and the great news is that it is not too late to cultivate empathy. If you're curious about your personal level of empathy, you can take the Empathy Quotient assessment found in the appendix. The Empathy Quotient,

---

[84] Lee, C.J. (2011). "Communication Competence, Empathy, and Self-Esteem." Journal of Humanities Therapy, 2, 83–94.

developed by Simon Baron-Cohen, is intended to measure how easily you pick up on other people's feelings, as well as how strongly you are affected by other's feelings.[85]

The secret to *positively influencing the next generation* begins with us—parents, youth pastors, teachers, counselors, and anyone who impacts the lives of youth. We have to master the skill of empathy so we can model and teach it to the next generation; they will not learn it from the Internet. It is through this developmental process that we become secure in our identity, not in the identity we create for others, but our identity in Christ. The more confident we are in who God called us to be, the easier it is for us to consolidate our perceived identities into one—the one that boldly proclaims, "This is who I am!"

---

[85] "The Empathy Quotient" (2011). Guardian News and Media Limited. Retrieved from https://www.theguardian.com/life/table/0,,937442,00.html

## 5  CHAPTER RECAP
# HIGHLIGHTS FROM "BINARY AND EMPATHY"

**Black-and-White Thinking.** Many people who use binary thinking get stuck in their black-and-white thinking, limited by their perceived choices, not aware of their available choices.

**Gray Thinking.** When we use binary or black-and-white thinking, we do not allow for open-minded learning and growth. We don't allow for the many shades of gray in our world.

**Binary Thinking and Addiction.** As addicts, we might think that black-and-white thinking keeps us safe, but really, it puts a choke hold on our sobriety; it is what keeps us in bondage.

**Disconnected.** While many researchers are concerned with how cell phone use affects childhood brain development, which is a valid concern, others are equally concerned with how cell phone use contributes to a lack of interaction between parents and children.

**How does shame develop?** There is a type of shame that is developed on an unconscious level and is the product of consistent negative attachment experiences, producing an emotional perspective not based on a person's behavior, but based on their perception of themselves.

**Shame and Relationships.** Shame has a way of distorting the perception of social interactions, making a benign situation appear negative. Continual misinterpretation of social situations—perceived as dismissive or rejection—creates a vicious cycle that negatively affects the ability to form relationships.

**The Unworthy Root.** As we ruminate over our imperfections and shortcomings, our feeling of shame distracts us from seeing ourselves objectively. At our core, we believe that we are unworthy—that we are worthless.

**Creating a Sense of Value.** It is imperative that parents learn to listen and understand their child's experiences in order for children to create a healthy sense of value. In many ways, a child's sense of self and value is rooted in connection.

**Parental Vulnerability.** As parents, we need to be emotionally vulnerable and let our children see us experience joy, love, excitement, sadness, pain, and disappointment. Our children learn empathy by observing and responding to our emotional experiences.

**The Internet and Identity.** When it comes to social media, young people are faced with amazing pressure—the pressure to be someone they're not. At some point, their profile no longer represents who they are on the inside, but represents who they think they have to be for their online friends and followers.

**Who I Am?** It is through this developmental process that we become secure in our identity, not in the identity we create for others, but our identity in Christ.

# IS THERE AN APP FOR THAT?

## NERD ALERT! _

We are ready to delve into the nuts and bolts of the available apps and tools that help reinforce accountability and healthy Internet use. As we walk through different concepts and ideas, I will be using terms that you may have heard or, perhaps, they are new to you. I will be providing brief descriptions of the technical terms as they are used. Additionally, there is a full list of terms and definitions in the glossary of the appendix.

Many of the definitions of terms used in this chapter are my own *simplified* definitions, written for the scope of this book, recognizing they may not be the most technically accurate definition of the term. My goal is to weed through all the techno-jargon and get down to the necessary elements so that anyone—you, your kids, and youth with whom you have influence—can create a healthy Internet Use Plan. We will explore the concepts of filtering, accountability, and monitoring. In the next chapter we'll look at practical ways to put everything in motion.

## I'LL HAVE WHAT HE'S HAVING _

One of my favorite parts of working at Pure Desire is having the opportunity to travel to churches across the country. I love meeting group members and leaders, hearing about the hope and freedom they've experienced as they engage in vulnerable accountability with their local group. As the resident nerd on the speaking team, during the Q & A sessions, most of the Internet-related questions seem to land in my direction. By far, the most common question they ask me is, "What accountability program do you use?" They want to know what I use for myself and my family. Because it must be what the experts use, it must be the best.

I've been asked this question enough times to realize, what they are really asking is: "What accountability app or filter should I use for myself and my family?" They think that if I use what the experts use and it's the best, it will be good enough for them too. Although this may seem like a simple and common question, the subject of filtering and accountability is anything but simple.

As we have discussed in previous chapters, the Internet is much more than a series of computers, networks, and services that exist for communication, information, social interaction, and consumption. It is infinitely complex and generally serves the designers rather than the consumers. To put it simply, users are at a technological disadvantage. There is no singular solution to support responsible Internet use for each and every user.

My typical answer to the question, "What accountability program do you use?" sounds something like this: Unfortunately there is no one-size-fits-all approach to Internet accountability. The Internet is broad, used in many different ways on many different devices. What works for me and my family may not be a good fit for yours. Responsible Internet use can't be summed up by finding the right app or using certain devices. It's about cultivating healthy online systems and behaviors.

Galatians 6:7 tells us that every person will reap what he (or she) sows. Anyone who desires to use the Internet responsibly should have these four basic elements as part of their Internet Use Plan. I like to use the acronym FARM to remember these four elements that are critical when cultivating healthy Internet use:

**F**iltering for any app or site likely to present content that is counter the user's values.

**A**ccountability for every device and connection in use.

**R**eview of the first two elements both periodically and anytime a new site, app, device, or connection is introduced.

**M**onitoring includes at least two other people that the user trusts, with whom they can be open and honest.

Essentially, what every person needs is a personally tailored plan for their Internet use. Even within my own family, each of us has a uniquely different plan that has been developed to fit how each of us uses the Internet. For the most part, we all use the same Internet connection (same ISP—Internet service provider), we share many of the same devices (TV, computers, game console), but, at the same time, there are many differences. All of us have different mobile devices (smartphones and tablets), we connect to different public networks (school, work, library, friend's house, airports, retail stores, coffee shops), and we have different app-specific accounts (social, gaming, work, school). All of these variations are expressions of each family member's interests, relationships, and how they connect in their daily routine.

By the end of this chapter, my goal is that you will have a solid understanding of these four elements, as well as the knowledge required to put your own Internet Use Plan in place. Let's start by looking at each of the four elements that are essential to every healthy Internet Use Plan and the practical steps to putting a plan together.

When helping others develop an Internet Use Plan (especially youth with whom you have influence), it is important to keep this in mind: your goal is to help them develop their own plan, not dictate what things ought to go in their plan. My goal as a parent is that by the time my kids set out on their own, they will have gained the skills to evaluate apps, sites, services, devices, and connections to set a plan in place that will support healthy Internet use. It is not my job to dictate what decisions they will make. I want to lead by example. I want them to follow my example because they trust me, not because they fear me.

## FILTERS AND ACCOUNTABILITY APPS _

When most people think about the tools that promote healthy Internet use, filters and accountability apps come to mind. It's important to first understand the difference between the two and what they can and cannot do. A filter is a software application or network hardware that blocks unwanted content. An accountability app is a software application that records and reports to a predetermined group of users the online activity of each user.

A good analogy of the two would be like an airplane's radar and black box. In the same way modern commercial aircraft use radar to detect and avoid hazardous weather patterns, a filter's job is to detect and avoid hazardous content. In the same way the black box records data—recording all of the pilot's activities, as well the status of all of the aircraft's systems for future analysis—

an accountability app is designed to record all of the user's online activities for future analysis.

A filter helps users avoid harmful content and an accountability app supports a user's transparency with trusted people in their lives. Additionally, in the same way that the pilot has ultimate control over the aircraft—they can turn off the aircraft's transponder, and radar can be disabled or simply ignored—the user has control over their Internet use. There are no foolproof filters or accountability apps; every single one can be bypassed. The simplest way to bypass accountability or filtering software is to use a device without these systems in place.

## ❯ WOULD YOU LIKE INAPPROPRIATE CONTENT WITH THAT?

As we discussed earlier, the Internet wants to know everything about you so it can market targeted advertisements to you. One of the few benefits of this type of marketing is that advertisers don't simply want to know what piques your interest, they also want to know what you don't like. Internet companies want to know what you find offensive. The last thing they want is to show you something that would cause you to leave their site or uninstall their app. Most major app developers and website administrators have built into their platform the ability to filter out unwanted content or allow the user the ability to define what they do and do not want to see. Some examples of built-in filtering are:

- Google SafeSearch: when SafeSearch is on, it helps block explicit images, videos, and websites from Google Search results.

- YouTube restricted mode: an optional setting that helps screen out potentially mature content that may not be appropriate for all viewers.

- Facebook privacy settings—unfriending and reporting content: most social networks like Facebook allow the user significant control over their feed (the content that the social network presents to the user).

- Google Music—blocking explicit lyrics: Google's music service includes the option to block explicit songs played on its radio stations.

These are just a few examples of apps and sites that offer some level of content control. One of the most important questions to ask when evaluating an app or site for filtering is, "Where is the content coming from?" Many of the most popular sites and apps need no filtering; the user provides 100 percent of the content. Some examples of these sites are:

- Google Drive, Dropbox, and iCloud: apps for storing and sharing user's personal files.

- Online banking: contains only the user's financial information. Managed by bankers, people who are more likely to post erroneous surcharges than inappropriate content to your account.

- Google Calendar: populated with the user's agenda and invitations to events from close friends and associates.

- Health-tracking apps: gathering data from the user's input and wearable devices.

Although user-provided content apps are typically innocuous, many have sharing capabilities. It's important to pay attention to who you're sharing your data with and what data others share with you. Social media is another platform where users provide the bulk of the content. For every social and content-sharing app, look at the privacy settings to see who can be in your network and what restrictions can be put in place.

For instance, Facebook can be set to only allow friend requests from friends of friends. This means that the only people who can request access to your information are people your friends have friended (accepted into their social network). It's also important to remember that Facebook and other social networks decide which friends' content you are likely to see. Make sure to unfriend contacts whose values are in direct opposition to yours. Facebook pays attention to these social cues. They are less likely to recommend friending other users who have values that are contrary to yours or presenting ads and posts with which you disagree.

The most important idea to understand about using built-in filters and restrictions on apps and sites is that using them sends the developers a very clear message. You are telling Internet advertisers, in no uncertain terms, "I know you're going to advertise to me, just don't advertise pornography or content that is in direct opposition to my values."

## ❯ KNOW YOUR NETWORK

Whenever possible, filtering your Internet connection should be a priority. Many Local Area Networks (LAN) you connect to have a filtering ability. A LAN is the local network you use to gain access to the Internet. Most of us connect to LANs via WiFi (wireless network connection). Some examples of LANs are:

- The WiFi connection at the coffee shop
- Your Internet connection at work
- All of the devices connected to your Internet router or modem at home
- The public computers at the library

For most users, the LAN at their home is where the bulk of their Internet use takes place. A 2017 study conducted by the Pew Research Institute shows that even with the exponential growth of cellular data (users getting their Internet connection via their cellular network provider), less than 20 percent of smartphone users use their cellular data plan as a primary Internet connection.[86] The home connection is the most convenient and cost-effective access users have to the Internet.

Additionally, users have the most content control on their home network. Unfortunately, in my experience, most people I have talked to at Pure Desire events have no filtering on their home LAN. When I ask whether they filter their home connection or not, the most common responses I receive are, "No, I'm not tech savvy. I don't want to mess up my Internet connection" or "I didn't even know I could do that."

Filtering your home Internet connection is a fairly simple process if you understand some basics of Internet routing. Most Internet filtering at the LAN level takes place through the Domain Name Service (DNS). A DNS is a computer on the Internet that returns IP addresses (the digital location of the computer hosting a site or service) when a website is requested.

For example, if you type into your web browser the address www.puredesire.org, your device will send the DNS the web address www.puredesire.org and that DNS will return 23.227.38.64 (Pure Desire's IP address) so that your device knows where to gain connection to the site, service, or app. When you add filtering to your LAN, essentially you're changing the default DNS from your Internet Service Provider's (ISP's) DNS to one

---

[86] Pew Research Center (2017). "Internet/Broadband Fact Sheet." January 12. Retrieved from http://www.pewinternet.org/fact-sheet/internet-broadband/

that is set up to filter requests from your devices. There are a number of free or very cost-effective (a couple dollars per month) solutions available. The DNS filters that I recommend are:

- OpenDNS: www.opendns.com
- SafeDNS: www.safedns.com
- DNSFilter: www.dnsfilter.com

There are many other DNS providers available. I suggest these three because, in my experience, they are the most simple to set up. Regardless of which service you choose, I recommend using one that includes the following:

- Predefined blocking categories: pornography, nudity, sexually explicit content, online gambling, violent content, etc.

- Easy setup instructions: make sure they offer the information you need to set up your router or modem for the service.

- Custom blacklists and whitelists: a DNS's predefined categories may not cover every site you or your family would like to block. Additionally, they may block sites that you want access to. Puredesire.org is a good example of a site that is blocked from most DNSs because the site contains sexual content. DNSs are good at categorization, but not so good at deciding what is healthy and detrimental. Blacklists and whitelists allow you to more accurately configure DNS filtering. A blacklist is simply an additional list of sites you can add to the predefined categories of sites you want the DNS service to block. A whitelist is just the opposite: a list of sites that you want the DNS to allow access (like www.puredesire.org, of course).

If a site is on the whitelists, your LAN will have access to it even if it is in one of the predefined blocked categories you've specified.

If the sound of DNS configurations and customized blacklists and whitelists are a bit overwhelming, here are two suggestions:

1. Ask your kids for assistance. Most Gen Zs (especially teenagers) are incredibly tech-savvy. One way to know if this is a good option for your family is to answer the question: "When my computer breaks, who do I ask for help?" If the answer is your kids, this is probably a really good option. If you decide to go this route, make sure you're involved in the entire setup process. Ask a lot of questions, take good notes, and make sure the goal is transparent use for the whole family. DO NOT tell your kids, "Hey, I'm concerned about some of the content we encounter online. Will you set up this DNS filter thingy for me?" and then walk away. You are essentially putting your family in a high-performance sports car, handing the keys to your teenager and saying, "I trust you to make good decisions and keep us all safe." You need to be just as invested in setting up a filter as your teenager.

2. There are pre-configured devices that offer setup and ongoing support with their services. This is essentially a router that replaces your current router and is configured out of the box to start filtering for your family. Typically, there is some type of setup process; however, it is very straightforward and the manufacturer's support staff is available for setup help. The cost for these routers and ongoing service is more than DNS filtering services,

but still very affordable. Some good examples of pre-configured routers are:

**a.** CleanRouter: cleanrouter.com

**b.** Circle: meetcircle.com

**c.** Norton Core Secure Router: us.norton.com

In addition to your home network, you should take note of filtering (or lack of filtering) available on other network connections. In general, most public networks (retail stores, coffee shops, etc.) have no filtering. It is good to be aware of this and limit your Internet use on these types of networks to trusted sites that you know will not provide inappropriate content. For those who struggle with pornography use, public networks may need to be off-limits altogether until a period of sobriety has been established. Most business and educational connections offer filtering. I recommend checking with the system administrator at school or work to find out what (if any) type of content is filtered. This will raise your awareness to the potential vulnerabilities when connecting at these locations.

## ❯ DO YOU SEE WHAT I SEE?

In the same way there exists a wide variety of filtering services, there are just as many accountability applications. Choosing an accountability app—just like a filter—comes down to finding one that fits you and your family's needs. The apps that I most often recommend are:

- Accountable2You: www.accountable2you.com
- Ever Accountable: everaccountable.com
- Covenant Eyes: www.covenanteyes.com

Regardless of which accountability app you choose to use, I recommend using one that includes the following features:

- Compatibility: accountability apps need to be able to run and report activities from all your devices—smartphone, laptop, tablet, etc. If you find you have a device that is not supported, like a game console, you may want to set up parental controls to restrict Internet browsing on the game console.

- Easy-to-read reports: most accountability apps have sample reports to preview prior to signing up for their service or a trial period to see how the app works. It is important to talk to the people you have chosen to be a part of your accountability support and make sure they know how to read the reports generated by the app.

- Uninstall or bypass notifications: the application should report to all accountability partners if, for any reason, the application is uninstalled or turned off.

- Record app activity: many applications have built-in web browsing features. For this reason, the accountability app needs to be able to record all app functions. This is an area that is a problem for Apple mobile device users.

**NOTE to iPhone and iPad users:** the last item that I listed for accountability apps is not possible for IOS users—Apple currently does not allow any app to monitor another app. This doesn't mean you need to ditch your Apple device to have healthy online use. It does mean that you will need to take some additional steps when setting up your device for accountability. Make sure your accountability app provider has instructions available for setting up your device. The user should have their accountability partners present for the setup process; they will need to set the app install pass code. (This is different than your Apple ID or unlock code.) To have accountability on your IOS devices also means you will not be able to add apps without one of your accountability partners present. You can still be one of the cool kids with an iPhone; you just might want to make sure your accountability partners are iPhone users too. No iPhone user wants to hear an Android user go on and on about how much better their Samsung Galaxy is because they can install apps whenever they want.

## IT'S THE LATEST APP—ALL THE COOL KIDS HAVE IT! _

Since 2008, when Android and Apple released their app stores, mobile devices have never been the same. It's funny to think that less than 10 years ago, when you purchased a cell phone, whatever apps came preloaded on the device were probably the only apps you were going to use until you got a new device. I will grant you that, yes, there was Handango for all of you Blackberry and PalmPilot fans reading this book.

That said, the Android and Apple app stores were such a significant step forward in the evolution of mobile software that it's really hard to make comparisons between Handango's ever-popular Snake game (a simple game in which the user maneuvers a line that grows in length, with the line itself being a primary obstacle) and YouTube, Whatsapp, or Instagram. Apps are such an integral key to how our mobile world works. In the last five years, developers have gone to great lengths to make your mobile device just as capable of completing tasks and running applications as your laptop.

Understanding the convenience and power mobile apps provide to our digital world is key when looking at the Review element of the FARM acronym discussed earlier in this chapter. With the simplicity and ease of adding an app (assuming you're not an iPhone user who has to call their accountability partners every time they want to install an app), we can unconsciously expose ourselves to more than we realize. This is important to consider when adding apps to devices; what exposure to unwanted content are we adding as well? I have heard a number of stories from Pure Desire group members who added an app to their device, not realizing that the app had explicit content or the ability to browse the Internet outside of their default browser.

Reviewing your Internet Use Plan should happen on a regular basis. I recommend completing the Internet Use Plan and reviewing it with your accountability partners at least once every three months. A copy of the Internet Use Plan can be found in the appendix, as well as on the Pure Desire website: www.puredesire.org/tools. It's also a good idea to review your plan for any of the following reasons:

- Adding an app to a mobile device: prior to installation, read the full app description; and upon installation, take note of any permissions the app is requesting. It's important to know the app's capabilities and how it may affect your Internet Use Plan.

- New devices: a laptop, smartphone, game console, smart TV

- New network connection that you plan to use on a regular basis

- Joining a social network

- Finding yourself involved in online behavior that you previously committed to abstain from; or for someone who is struggling with addictive online behavior, when there is a lapse or relapse.

## TAP TAP TAP...IS THIS THING ON? _

Remember the FARM acronym? We have looked at Filtering, Accountability, and Review—all of which are crucial to healthy Internet use. The last piece needed in developing an Internet Use Plan is Monitoring. Of the four elements discussed, this is by far the most critical. Monitoring is where the user is able to receive feedback from people they have chosen to help keep them accountable. The goal of accountability is to be fully known, so that those who love and care about us can support our health and freedom. This means that your accountability partners are helping you see the holes in your Internet Use Plan; they are asking about questionable sites, apps, and online activity, identifying patterns that may be moving you away from healthy Internet use.

> YOU CAN'T MANAGE WHAT YOU DON'T MEASURE.
> PETER DRUCKER [87]

When I have the opportunity to meet with Pure Desire group leaders, I ask them, "What is the greatest challenge your group members experience when using accountability apps?" The most common response I've heard is the process of reading the reports—they don't know what to look for or feel overwhelmed: there is so much data included, they are not tech-savvy and don't feel qualified to provide feedback.

Reading reports for your accountability partners can feel daunting, but following a few basic rules can make it a very manageable process.

---

[87] Drucker, P. (1967). The Effective Executive: The Definitive Guide to Getting the Right Things Done. New York, NY: HarperCollins Publishers.

- Reading reports needs to happen on a weekly basis and should only take five to ten minutes. As an accountability partner, your job is to look through the report and simply ask questions. This is not a forensic investigation. The goal of the accountability report is transparency for the user. Most Pure Desire group members and youth who have used accountability apps with partners report, "Simply knowing my partner is looking at my report and asking questions significantly increases my awareness of what I choose to do online." If you find that the reports are regularly requiring you or your accountability partners to spend more than ten minutes per week to review, consider using a different accountability app with more streamlined reporting.

- Reading the reports needs to include...reading the report. I know this sounds obvious, but this is one of the most common steps that partners fail to complete. Frequently, accountability partners will receive an email summary of their partner's report, check to see that there are no highly questionable sites flagged in the email, hit the delete button on the email, and assume that they have done their job for the week. As an accountability partner you need to think of the email summary as a notification reminder to review the full online report. When you get an email notification, look for a link or button that will take you to the full report. In the full report there are four things you should be looking for:

  · Questionable sites: the accountability app should flag these sites. Don't attempt to follow the links to the sites or do research on the sites. Have a conversation with the user and ask the question, "Can you tell me what these questionable sites are and why you visited them?"

- Change in usage: some accountability apps show this in measurement of time and others show number records. If a user has dramatically changed their Internet usage (especially if it has decreased), this is something that should be discussed. Typically when this happens (especially with teenagers), it's not that they are using the Internet less, it's that they are using devices that are not connected to their accountability app. This could be intentional—the user is attempting to hide online behavior; however, it could also be unintentional— the user bought a new phone and forgot to set up the accountability software. Either way, you should not make assumptions. Just ask the question, "Can you tell me why your Internet use has changed?"

- New apps: Any time a new app appears on the report (especially one you're not familiar with), you should ask the user what the app does and how this app fits into their Internet Use Plan. Additionally, if there are apps on the report that are known to contain inappropriate content, a discussion about why those apps are being used needs to take place.

- Proxies and IP addresses: a proxy is another computer in the Internet that serves as a hub through which requests are processed. The proxy allows a user to request sites that the proxy displays for the user without filtering or reporting it to a user's accountability app. Usually, proxies will not be flagged by accountability apps as questionable; however, they will still show up in a report. To check to see if a proxy has been used you need to see the full report of all sites visited. Most accountability reports have the ability to create full reports. If it's not clear how to do this, contact the accountability app's tech support. Once you have the full report displayed, use your web browser's find feature and search for the word "proxy." If a user has been using a proxy, there will be a listing of a web searches that includes the word "proxy." In addition, you need to see if the user has tried to access a website with an IP address. This is where a user looks up the IP address of a website—without using the web browser or on an unprotected computer—then uses that IP address to gain access to a website without the URL being identified by the filter or accountability app. The easiest way to see if the user has been accessing web pages via an IP address is to scroll through the full report and look for four sets of numbers delimited by periods; 22.66.404.12. When scrolling through lists of websites, IP addresses are easy to spot; they are likely the only groups of numbers amid a bunch of text. If you find that the user has been using proxies or IP addresses, this is also a good time to have a conversation.

When it comes to healthy Internet use and creating an Internet Use Plan, bringing all of the elements of the FARM approach together can result in some great conversations with your family and the youth with whom you have influence. Remember, let the user own the process; let them make the decisions about how involved they're going to be with setting up filters and accountability programs.

Accountability apps are often used with the best intent, but frequently not used to their fullest potential. Users set up an accountability app, add partners, and then nothing happens. They continually question whether the app is doing its job, when really, it's more of an operator error. As an accountability partner, your role is simple: don't play investigator; review the full report; take notes; and ask good questions. Most importantly, be consistent. At least once a week, take the time to review the reports and have the necessary conversations required for support and maintaining health.

We covered many technical aspects of Internet use, all of which are important for developing an Internet Use Plan. Remember, if you get bogged down by the techno-jargon, refer to the glossary in the appendix. Now, you're ready to put all of these tools into practice.

## CHAPTER RECAP
### 6 HIGHLIGHTS FROM "IS THERE AN APP FOR THAT?"

**Responsible Internet Use.** The Internet is much more than a series of computers, networks, and services that exist for communication, information, social interaction, and consumption. It is infinitely complex and generally serves the designers rather than the consumers. To put it simply, users are at a technological disadvantage.

**Filters and Accountability Apps.** A filter is a software application or network hardware that blocks unwanted content. An accountability app is a software application that records and reports to a predetermined group of users the online activity of each user.

**Built-in Filtering.** Most major app developers and website administrators have built into their platform the ability to filter out unwanted content or allow the user the ability to define what they do and do not want to see.

**No Filtering?** Many of the most popular sites and apps need no filtering; the user provides 100 percent of the content. Social media is a platform where users provide the bulk of the content.

**Sharing Capabilities.** It's important to pay attention to who you are sharing your data with and what data others share with you.

**Local Area Networks.** Many Local Area Networks (LAN) you connect to have a filtering ability. A LAN is the local network you use to gain access to the Internet. For most users, the LAN at their home is where the bulk of their Internet use takes place.

**Accountability Partners.** Monitoring is where the user is able to receive feedback from people they have chosen to help keep them accountable. The goal of accountability is to be fully known, so that those who love and care about us can support our health and freedom.

**Creating an Internet Use Plan.** When it comes to healthy Internet use and creating an Internet Use Plan, bringing all of the elements of the FARM approach together can result in some great conversations with your family and the youth with whom you have influence.

# | TOOLS AND RULES

## ADOPT-A-FAMILY? _

For anyone who grew up in a military or ministry family, there is a decent chance that more than once in your childhood you packed up everything and moved to a different town. Given that my father was not only a Marine but also a pastor, as a child, I was quite good at packing up, moving to a different town, making new friends, and adopting family.

That's what we called it: "adopting family." This was how my family of origin described making close friends at church and school that we would treat like family—hanging out on holidays and special occasions in lieu of having actual extended family close. In addition to packing up and moving thirteen times by the time I was ten years old, we didn't have much extended family. On my dad's side, he had seven physically abusive stepfathers and his mom passed away shortly after I was born. On my mom's side, her parents rarely visited and her only brother had a busy career and no children.

I'm happy to say that these days my family is much more extensive. When I married my wife, I inherited more cousins, uncles, and aunts than I can keep straight. My kids have two sets of grandparents, a bunch of uncles and aunts, and dozens of cousins who we spend holidays and special occasions with. As much as I appreciate adopted family, having extended family I get to see regularly is so enjoyable. My sister and I have both been very fortunate to have our parents live close and our kids experience the joy of hanging out with Grandma and Grandpa on a regular basis.

One of the unexpected elements of having kids and extended family close are house rules. Although my parents and my sister have very similar values to my wife and me, there are always slight differences in how each family decides to create order within their house.

On many occasions when my kids were little, in protest to one of our house rules, they would say, "But Grandma lets me do that at her house!" or "Grandpa lets me have dessert even if I don't finish my dinner!" I would try to convince my kids that Grandpa and Grandma weren't so nice or lenient when I was growing up. I would tell them, "These are two old people who are trying to get into heaven." I don't think my kids ever believed me. They often responded with, "We want to live at Grandma and Grandpa's house!"

One time when my niece Ashley was very young, my sister caught her jumping on one of their beds. She quickly corrected her saying, "Ashley! We don't jump on the bed." Ashley replied, "I can jump on the bed at Grandma's house." My sister told her, "That might be true at Grandma's house, but at this house, there is absolutely no jumping on the bed!" Ashley replied, "Where did we get this house anyway?"

When my sister told me that story, I remember thinking how imaginative my niece's perspective was on the world, especially at her age. She must have thought that when her parents were house-hunting, the listing for the house they purchased would have read:

*Beautiful 3-bedroom, 2-bath house, in a quiet neighborhood. Gas furnace, 2-car garage, city water and sewer, and ABSOLUTELY NO JUMPING ON THE BED!*

Although the story of my niece's perspective is quite comical—regarding the challenges real estate agents face when selling a house with a "no jumping on the bed" ordinance—it underlines a valuable point: rules are a necessary part of living in relationship. Rules define how we relate to one another, how we show respect and value for others, how we respect ourselves, and how we relate to our Heavenly Father. Whether you're the type of person who appreciates the predictability and order of a world with rules or more of a free spirit who would prefer to create their own rules—or have none at all—the inescapable truth is that God designed our world with rules.

## EVEN ANARCHISTS HAVE RULES _

Any quest for truth—through scientific experiment, a philosophical debate, or spending time in God's Word—is an endeavor that will inevitably lead us back to a greater understanding of God and the amazing world He created. Whether it is the laws of Newtonian physics, quantum mechanics, or the Ten Commandments, all are rules that have been found to be consistently true within the realm of human existence. When they are followed, they make our relationship with God and others beneficial. Not understanding or choosing to ignore the rules by which our world operates creates isolation from God and others.

In the last chapter, we discussed the necessary elements to developing healthy online behaviors with the Internet Use Plan. When implemented, the Internet Use Plan contains rules that we agree to follow so we can develop healthy online behavior. In this chapter, we will look at how to best put those rules in motion. As parents, grandparents, youth leaders, teachers, and individuals who have influence on the next generation, the way in which we implement and enforce rules is often more important than the rule itself.

## I PREFER TO ISOLATE BY MYSELF _

Rules without relationship leads to isolation. Isolation leads us away from growth and maturity. As we have previously discussed, there are some striking similarities between teens and addicts in this sense. Both teens and addicts lack a sufficient capacity for higher reasoning and are generally more impulsive compared to adults with a fully developed brain who are not experiencing addictive behaviors. When working with individuals who struggle with destructive behaviors, it seems like human nature to put rigid structures in place (especially for those who lack impulse control). Unfortunately, this approach is more likely to yield the exact opposite of the desired outcome. One of the most obvious examples of rules with minimal relationship is found in the United States Correctional System.[88] The United States has the largest population of incarcerated criminals, yet we have unbelievably high recidivism rates: the rate of rearrest.[89]

- Within one year of release, more than half (56.7 percent) of released prisoners are rearrested by the end of the first year.

---

[88] Schmalleger, F. (2014). *Criminal Justice: A Brief Introduction* (10th ed.). Upper Saddle River, NJ: Pearson Education, Inc.

[89] Carey, Jesse (2015). "America's Criminal Justice System Is Broken." Relevant. Retrieved from https://relevantmagazine.com/reject-apathy/12-stats-show-how-broken-americas-criminal-justice-system.

- Within three years of release, about two-thirds (67.8 percent) of released prisoners are rearrested.

- Within five years of release, about three-quarters (76.6 percent) of released prisoners are rearrested.

As a nation, we have become proficient at creating consequences to enforce our rules. The issue is not so much the rules and enforcement as it is the lack of relationship and rehabilitation for those who violate the rules. There is a significant difference between punishment and allowing people to feel the weight of their choices, while simultaneously feeling the support of people who care about them.

God's purpose for rules is to become conscious of our conscience. Gaining a clear sense of right and wrong (conscience) can only happen when we are emotionally invested in others and how they feel (being conscious). All too often, we tend to believe that people who constantly make bad choices are bad people or that bad people are a result of bad choices. The Bible clearly states that this idea is totally false.

*For all have sinned and fall short of the glory of God.*
ROMANS 3:23

There are no good people or bad people; there are just sinners. Every single one of us sinners is incapable of following all the rules. Jesus uses the analogy of the vine and its branches to emphasize the significance of our relationship with Him:

*I am the vine; you are the branches. Whoever abides in me*
*and I in him, he it is that bears much fruit,*
*for apart from me you can do nothing.*
JOHN 15:5 (ESV)

When humans isolate (especially from God), we literally cannot help but sin. We are incapable of following God's rules without relationship. This is not just a theological perspective, it is a universal truth that scientists and psychologists have found to be consistently true.

## THE HAPPIEST PLACE ON EARTH... FOR A RAT _

In the late 1970s, a Canadian psychologist, Bruce Alexander, wanted to understand why the current approach (at that time) to addiction recovery was having such minimal success.[90] Prior to Alexander's work, much of the laboratory testing related to substance abuse had been repeated with clear and obvious conclusions: *drugs create addictive behaviors; addicts are generally helpless to change those addictive behaviors; therefore, intervening with a rigid rehab program with strict relational consequences was the only way to experience change.* Although these conclusions led to minimal rehabilitation rates, they did appear to explain the outcome of the experiments. This is where Alexander's work came into the picture. He begin to wonder if the results of the experiment were more about the design of the experiment than the effects of the substances (drugs) being tested.

Prior to his research, drug addiction experiments generally used the same approach: get a lab rat, a cage, food, water, and an unlimited supply of a drug, such as heroin. The experiment was extremely replicable. Almost 100 percent of the test subjects (rats), when put in the cage with a choice of food, water, and

---

[90] Alexander, B. (2010). "Addiction: The View from Rat Park." Retrieved from http://www.brucekalexander.com/articles-speeches/rat-park/148-addiction-the-view-from-rat-park.

heroin, would either overdose on heroin or die of starvation as the result of only using the drug and not eating or drinking. The conclusion was simple: rat plus heroin equals addiction and death. For all you math nerds: Rats + Heroin = Addiction + Death. The experiment appeared to also explain the human behavior of heroin addicts: human plus heroin equals addiction and death.

There was one problem. There were some real-world anomalies. For instance: at the time, it was common practice for patients who had a major surgery (like a joint replacement) to take Diamorphine, prescribed for pain management during recovery. Diamorphine is a prescription version of heroin, typically a more pure form than the illegal street version. If the laboratory drug test on rats was accurate, when Grandpa had his hip replaced and took his doctor-prescribed Diamorphine during recovery, in no time at all, Grandpa would become a raging heroin addict. But that wasn't the case. Grandpa took his meds, rested, and over the course of several weeks with the help of physical therapy, he regained mobility. He no longer needed heroin to manage his pain and get through the day.

Alexander began to wonder why the real-world application didn't always match the experiment (especially with prescription medication). He wondered: perhaps it's not the heroin or substance that creates the addiction. In the experiment, it was assumed that the drug was the source of addictive behavior, given that it was the only foreign element (not normally part of a rat's environment).

However, Alexander observed that the cage was also foreign to a rat's natural environment. What if the cage was the source of the addiction and not the substance? He decided to modify the experiment by removing the cage. He maintained all of the foundational elements of the experiment (food, water, and heroin) and in place of the cage, created a large enclosure that was essentially Rat Disneyland. He called the environment Rat Park. In addition to removing the cage, Alexander added rat entertainment: treadmills, balls, tunnels, other rat toys, and most importantly, other rats. There were boundaries to keep the rats contained, but containment really wasn't much of an issue. The rats appeared to be having a great time with the toys and all of their rat friends.

Alexander and others repeated this experiment for a number of years and their findings were astounding.[91] In Rat Park, he observed that the rats rarely used the readily available heroin, and they never used the heroin habitually. Furthermore, since the initial Rat Park experiments, several experiments have pointed to the development of addictive behaviors in rats who are simply confined to a cage with food and water. Evidence suggests,

### THE OPPOSITE OF ADDICTION IS NOT SOBRIETY. THE OPPOSITE OF ADDICTION IS CONNECTION.[92]

The conclusion that isolation has destructive effects on humans should not surprise us. We know that the worst form of incarceration is solitary confinement; however, when evaluating societal norms, isolation is commonly utilized in attempt to correct behavior. When an addict is out of control, it is common to have an intervention, where the people who love and care about the addict say they've had enough and threaten to cut off relationship if the person doesn't shape up immediately!

[91] Hartman, P. (2015). "Everything You Know About Addiction Is Wrong." Childhood Obesity News. Retrieved from http://childhoodobesitynews.com/2015/06/11/everything-you-know-about-addiction-is-wrong/.

[92] Hari, J. (2016). *Chasing the Scream: The First and Last Days of the War on Drugs*. New York, NY: Bloomsbury Publishing.

We incarcerate teenagers dealing drugs who grew up outside a healthy family system. We threaten to lock down the Internet (Gen Z's primary connection to the world around them) when our kids use it inappropriately. All too often, when helping broken people, we end up creating further damage by removing relationship and connection—the most critical element of change.

Don't get me wrong, some of our actions should definitely have consequences. People who have violated children should not have access to children. People who have committed violent crimes should not be allowed to have weapons. Yes, clear boundaries related to destructive behaviors must be put in place for the safety of all those involved.

At the same time, people need the support of those around them when working to see transformation take shape in their lives. The problem is that negative behavior never affects just the person behaving negatively. Our choices always affect the people around us. This makes setting healthy boundaries challenging. My good friend, Nick Stumbo, describes the challenge this way: hurt people, hurt people; and healed people, heal people. Meaning that we are imperfect, sinful people in whom God abides. We have all wounded others out of our own woundedness and, at the same time, we all have the capacity to help others in their healing process as we reflect the grace and truth of what God has done in our lives.

You may be asking yourself, "What does this have to do with keeping my kids safe from pornography?" Frankly, a lot. As we have discussed, the Internet is pervasive in our society. There is no caging or containing the Internet. Creating rigid punitive rules for our kids' Internet use will only create more isolation, removing them further from support and reality. There is always another unprotected, unfiltered device somewhere—at the library or a friend's house—ready to provide isolation.

If we create an environment of rigid disengagement with a long list of things not to do, eventually the very rules that we have established for our kids' protection will drive them further into isolation. I know that, just like me, my kids are not perfect— they will struggle to always make the right decision. My goal in parenting is to foster an environment where our relationship is the focus, not all of their mistakes. If we want to see change for the next generation, we must implement an Internet Use Plan with relationship in mind.

I want to suggest four key elements to creating rules that will empower your kids to make great choices: shared values; leading by example; feeling the weight of decisions; and fostering relationship.

## ❯ SHARED VALUES

In the appendix, we have included a tool called the Family Values Exercise. It is designed to help families make some positive changes through the process of developing healthy Internet behaviors, allowing all members to have input in decisions and gain ownership of the outcome. When healthy values are internalized, kids will take those values into adulthood. This is also a very effective tool to use in a small group setting. When working with youth, it's a great way for them to understand how the choices we make affect our relationship with others.

I would encourage you to plan an evening with your family, or small group, to work through the exercise. In the exercise, each member creates a collage that identifies what they personally value. As a group, share the collages and ask the group to identify values that are common within the whole group. Next, create a list of at least five (but not more than ten) values that are agreed upon or shared among the group. Finally, discuss the behaviors that support or violate those values and the consequences connected to those behaviors. Ask these questions:

- What are the natural consequences that will happen when our values are violated?

- What are the rewards for supporting these values?

It is really important to keep two things in mind during this part of the exercise (especially as a parent): as much as possible, ask questions, and make sure the group values apply to everyone (parents and leaders included). This is a great opportunity for kids to understand that rules and consequences exist to help us change and grow.

We have previously discussed the importance of a child's identity—where it comes from and how it is developed over time. Establishing shared values is an important aspect of forming and contributing to one's identity. Recent research suggests that 71 percent of parents say they have a specific set of values that indicate and support behavior, but less than one-third (only 27 percent) have written out their shared values.[93] If the family values are only determined and known by the parents, how does a child identify with or take on those values as their own? How do they influence a child's identity? Through the Family Values Exercise and the Internet Use Plan you will have the opportunity to create (to write down) shared values that represent the collective attitudes, actions, and behaviors of the entire family.

Shared values are imperative within a family or small group. Without them it is impossible to create healthy boundaries. Every member has a different idea of what is healthy, especially when it

---

[93] Barna (2017). "Forming Family Values in a Digital Age." Barna Group Inc. Retrieved from https://www.barna.com/research/forming-family-values-digital-age/.

comes to Internet use, as well as deciding what should be filtered, what devices to use, and what content we value. Additionally, the Family Values Exercise will help determine what are the agreed upon consequences for violating or upholding our values. When these values are agreed-upon first, implementing an Internet Use Plan becomes much more doable. The family has determined what is appropriate, what is inappropriate, and what the related consequences are. This moves the role of mom and dad, or small group leader, from dictating the rules to supporting the decided-upon values. The rules become a reflection of the shared values.

## ❯ LEADING BY EXAMPLE

One of the most important ways you can help kids make wise choices is to demonstrate those decisions in your own life. This is not a call to parents and leaders to seek perfection or project the perception that, somehow, you have it all together. Whether you realize it or not, your kids already know you are far from perfect. The goal is honest vulnerable transparency. Once shared values are implemented (from the Family Values Exercise), accepting consequences when you violate those values is the most powerful way to communicate to your kids: *change happens when we live in community and accept how our behaviors affect those we care about.*

As a parent or leader, if you are struggling to maintain healthy online behavior, you need to be actively seeking help. This doesn't mean that you need to confess the details of your struggle to your kids and the youth you influence. They just need to know that you are human too and are taking the necessary steps to see transformation in your own life. This might mean that you (and your spouse, if you're married) need to be in a Pure Desire group.

Regardless of whether or not you are personally struggling with online behavior, you should have your own personal Internet Use Plan. I recommend completing it with your kids as they complete their plan. It is important to communicate that **everyone** needs an Internet Use Plan in place. Everyone needs to own and respect the family's values.

## ❯ FEELING THE WEIGHT OF DECISIONS

Frequently, when imposing consequences (especially as parents), we tend to focus on correcting the problem at hand and overlook the opportunity to allow our kids to feel the consequences of their choices. This means that discipline becomes more about understanding how our behaviors affect others than the consequences that we feel. When it is identified that someone in the family has violated a shared value, we need to first understand who else was affected by the violation and what needs to be done to repair the relationship. Then ask the question: what are the consequences relating to that behavior?

Here is an example:

*The family has a shared value of face-to-face conversation and identified that bringing a cell phone to the dinner table violates that value. When a family member forgets or ignores this value, the consequence is no screen time for the rest of the day. One of the kids is texting a friend as they sit down at the table. Instead of saying, "Hey, no phones at the table! You've lost screen time for the rest of the day," ask two questions: 1—How do you think the rest of the family feels when you sit down at the dinner table texting on your phone; what is the message you are sending the rest of the family? 2—What does our family values chart say about bringing our phone to the table?*

It is so important to help kids develop empathy, especially when consequences are implemented. When we experience life's consequences and do not understand how others are affected, we are more likely to become resentful of the consequence and miss the opportunity for growth.

As a parent, modeling this process is critical. When my kids point out that I have violated one of the family's values, I need to recognize that the way I respond will significantly affect how likely they will accept the consequences of their own behavior. When my kids say, "Hey Dad, you're violating our family values! You're not allowed to have your phone at the dinner table," if I become defensive and make excuses for my behavior, saying, "I'm the parent and that was an important work call," I am communicating that not only are the family's values not important, but that work is more important than my family. As a parent, this is a crucial place to show humility, supporting the family's values, recognizing how my behaviors make others feel, and gladly accepting the consequences of my actions. This will lead the way for my kids to do the same.

## ❯ FOSTERING RELATIONSHIP

This last element is probably the most challenging, as it often requires a good deal of creativity and awareness. Fostering relationship is about utilizing both consequence and reward to increase connection. The goal is not to only maintain connection between the parent or group leader and a kid. It is about fostering relationship among the entire family or group, creating unity and a oneness among all members. Too often, we unintentionally make use of consequences and rewards that create isolation and separation within the family or group.

We have to be intentional about fostering relationship. Here's an example: When siblings are fighting, most parents will separate the kids. This may stop the fighting, but it doesn't allow the kids to learn how to develop healing in community. As a child, when I fought with my sibling, we were not separated, but put in a room together. What's worse is that we couldn't leave the room until we had restored the relationship. Sometimes, this took hours. This practice of facilitating connection didn't stop there. When I had a friend over, and my friend and I behaved negatively toward my sibling, immediately the friend went home and I went to a room with my sibling to restore the relationship. My parents were intentional about fostering relationship—it was a core component to our shared values. Now, as a parent, I use this same strategy to foster relationship among my kids.

It is important to be careful when rewarding behavior; it promotes shared values to reward the family and not the individual. If we only reward the individual for their efforts, we can unintentionally communicate to the rest of the family or group that there is a hierarchy among its members, causing them to think: *I can never get it right, or I don't have it all together like my siblings or parents.*

Rewards should incorporate the collective efforts of the family or group. As parents or leaders, this means that we must be aware of even the slightest behavioral improvements that support the family's values. Perhaps it's simply a reduction in negative behaviors. Maybe your teenager is constantly condescending and sarcastic (especially toward their siblings), but this week, they have generally been more respectful to family members—not perfect, but making progress. This is noteworthy and cause for celebration! When there is a family reward, such as going out to dinner, be sure to point out how each member contributed to the shared value, no matter how minimal the input of some may have been.

Consequences can also be divisive in how the family relates. When we feel the weight of consequences, it is human nature to withdraw or isolate. Although a consequence may result in a boundary that is put in place to protect those who have been violated by our poor choices, the goal of a consequence is to learn from our mistakes in community. As Christ-followers, Paul instructs us to experience life in this way together:

> *Rejoice with those who rejoice; mourn with those who mourn. Live in harmony with one another. Do not be proud, but be willing to associate with people of low position. Do not be conceited.*
> ROMANS 12:15-16

Paul is clear: whether we are rejoicing over the rewards of living by our values or suffering the consequences that come from behaviors that violate our values, community is necessary. As parents and leaders, it is not our job to dole out punishment; we are called to support each other in difficult times, even if the difficulty is self-inflicted. When my son loses screen time because he has been rude in how he relates to Mom, this is my job: I want to help him see that because he is spending too much time on his device, he has become self-focused and not sensitive to those around him. Additionally, I what him to know that I understand what it feels like to lose privileges. I want him to know that he is loved and valuable. I will often say, "I know you're bummed that there is no Minecraft today. I get it. I'd be bummed too; but the good news is that you now have time to head out to the backyard with me and throw the football."

Fostering relationship in a family or small group is hard work. It requires investment, humility, and a ton of patience. If I am honest, as a parent, I rarely pull it off. I know that in the same way I do my best to show grace and mercy to my kids, my Heavenly Father abundantly and overwhelmingly shows me His grace and mercy.

One of my favorite quotes about family is from my dad:

**MARRIAGE IS GOD'S GREAT PLAN TO GROW YOU UP...
AND IF THAT DOESN'T WORK, HE GIVES YOU KIDS.**

After 21 years of marriage and two kids, I wholeheartedly agree. I never knew how much I needed to grow until I had a family of my own.

What we now understand about human behavior, and rat behavior, is that isolation leads to addictive behaviors. It is in relationship that we develop healthy behaviors and thrive. When it comes to keeping kids safe on the Internet, they need to have a realistic Internet Use Plan with rules that reflect relationship. Provide healthy suggestions and support as you together develop shared values that foster relationship and connectedness. As we look to what the future holds, help your kids, and those you influence, make wise choices about their online behavior.

## 7

### CHAPTER RECAP
# HIGHLIGHTS FROM "TOOLS AND RULES"

**Rules and Relationship.** Rules are a necessary part of living in relationship. Rules define how we relate to one another, how we show respect and value for others, how we respect ourselves, and how we relate to our Heavenly Father.

**Isolating Alone.** Rules without relationship leads to isolation. Isolation leads us away from growth and maturity.

**Feeling Our Mistakes.** There is a significant difference between punishment and allowing people to feel the weight of their choices, while simultaneously feeling the support of people who care about them.

**Drug Addiction Experiments.** Many of the laboratory tests related to substance abuse have been repeated with clear and obvious conclusions: *drugs create addictive behaviors; addicts are generally helpless to change those addictive behaviors; therefore, intervening with a rigid rehab program with strict relational consequences was the only way to experience change.*

**The Cage of Isolation.** Alexander observed that the cage was also foreign to a rat's natural environment. What if the cage was the source of the addiction and not the substance?

**Rat Disneyland?** Alexander created a large enclosure that was essentially Rat Disneyland. He called the environment Rat Park. In addition to removing the cage, he added rat entertainment: treadmills, balls, tunnels, other rat toys, and most importantly, other rats.

**Isolation and Addiction.** The conclusion that isolation has destructive effects on humans should not surprise us. We know that the worst form of incarceration is solitary confinement; however, when evaluating societal norms, isolation is commonly utilized in attempts to correct behavior.

**Caging the Internet.** There is no caging or containing the Internet. Creating rigid punitive rules for our kids' Internet use will only create more isolation, removing them further from support and reality.

**Creating Shared Values.** Shared values are imperative within a family or small group. Without them it is impossible to create healthy boundaries. Every member has a different idea of what is healthy, especially when it comes to Internet use.

**Consequence and Reward.** Fostering relationship is about utilizing both consequence and reward to increase connection. Too often, we unintentionally make use of consequences and rewards that create isolation and separation within the family or group.

# WHAT THE FUTURE HOLDS

## PREDICTING THE PAST IS MUCH EASIER THAN THE FUTURE ___

As stated several times within the previous chapters, our goal is to answer the question: *How can we positively influence the next generation?* How can we help guide the youth who we influence in making wise online decisions? With that purpose in mind, I felt it necessary to not only explore the current reality of the Internet today, but additionally, do my best to identify what the future of the Internet holds. What new challenges to healthy Internet use is new technology likely to create? That said, I admit, I'm apprehensive about writing this final chapter. I have an overwhelming fear that years from now, like Steven Spielberg, I will receive letters from frustrated readers asking, "Where is my hoverboard or that flying car you promised? And why can't I power the flying car that doesn't exist with garbage?"

Hopefully, as I proceed with my future predictions, you—the reader—will be gracious if I mention some truly amazing emerging technology that does not come to fruition. Additionally, if copies of this book still exist in the year 2030 (assuming that people still read books in 2030), please do your best to refrain from laughing out loud or making comments to your friends like, "You'll never believe what they thought the future would be like way back in 2017!"

My hope is in that in this concluding chapter, you will not only get a glimpse of what the future of the Internet may hold, but more importantly, you'll have an opportunity to ponder future implications. This is a practice that I have personally found to have great value. Aside from being a nerd who loves all things tech (especially new tech), considering what is to come is a great avenue for engaging conversations with the youth I influence. It can be an open door to helping them consider how technology is changing our world and how we, as followers of Christ, can respond proactively.

If you are not someone who stays current on new technology, I would recommend checking out and possibly subscribing to one or more of the following sites. They are great sources for additional information pertaining to all the new tech that I discuss in this chapter:

- cnet.com
- mashable.com
- theverge.com
- techcrunch.com

## MORE OF THE SAME _

Before looking at the latest and greatest new technology, I want to point out that you can expect the elements that currently drive the Internet, which we discussed in chapter 1, to continue to grow in scale and have significant impact on Gen Z and future generations to come.

Internet access is expected to exceed 80 percent of the world's population by the year 2030.[94] By the year 2020, it is estimated that the Internet will have 10 times the amount of data. To put that number into perspective, if you recall the analogy used to describe how much data is currently on the Internet—a stack of iPads stretching past the orbit of the International Space Station—by the year 2020, that stack would reach the moon six times! Why so much data in such a short amount of time? The estimate is based on the number of Internet users who are currently ditching local storage on their computers for the convenience of having all of their data online.

Technological convergence—the concept that every device is connected to the Internet and will uniquely communicate information to the user—will also continue to accelerate in growth. In the very near future, just about every device that uses electricity will be online. When my wife and I were at the big-box store in search of a replacement for our ailing refrigerator, we were shocked to come across a WiFi-enabled model. Through a set of cameras and a built-in computer, the refrigerator will manage the expiration date of foods, create a shopping list, and for those really on-the-go folks, it will order groceries to be delivered to your front door. This tech is available today and will only become more common.

## LATEST AND GREATEST _

Looking at the time, energy, and money tech companies spend on research and development, there is enough content to write a

---

[94] Krishnan, M. (2014). "How Many People Will Have Internet Access by 2020 and 2030?" Retrieved from https://www.quora.com/How-many-people-will-have-internet-access-by-2020-and-2030.

multi-volume series on emerging technology that is likely to affect our lives in the next 10 years. For that reason, I want to narrow the scope. I will only be looking at technology that accelerates the essence of the Internet—Anything, Anytime, Anywhere—and technology that already, in some form, has hit the market. To help evaluate how these new offerings will affect us, I will be grouping them into two categories: Quantum Computing and Augmented Reality.

## SCHRÖDINGER'S CAT WALKS INTO A BAR AND DOESN'T _

Whether you have ever heard of quantum computing or not, if you're like me, just trying to wrap my brain around the title "Quantum Computing" makes my head hurt. Of the two categories we will discuss, quantum computing is the more complex and not intuitive. For that reason, I'm not going to spend much time trying to explain this technology. Rather, I will approach this topic in general terms and analogies. Don't worry, I won't even mention superposition of quantum states of entangled particles.

Let's start by looking at the basic difference between a conventional computer and a quantum computer. Then we'll look at what the applications are and how they might affect our kids and future generations. Looking at the most basic element of a computer's processor, its function hasn't changed much since Bell Labs created the TRADIC computer in 1954 (the first transistorized computer in the U.S.).[95] The computer as a whole

---

[95] Flamm, K. (1988). *Creating the Computer: Government, Industry and High Technology.* Washington, DC: The Brookings Institution.

has changed significantly; the TRADIC was the size of a large room and had less processing power than a basic calculator.

The most basic element of a conventional computer— the transistor—has essentially provided computers the same function for the last 60 years. It's just become a lot smaller. A computer's processor is basically a collection of billions of these transistors. In the 1950s, a single transistor was about the size of a pencil eraser. Today, you can fit billions of transistors in a single processor chip the size of a pencil eraser; hence, the modern computer is no longer the size of a room.

A conventional computer uses transistors to create two states for computation. These two states relate to the transistor being either turned on or off. Computers see these states numerically as a 1 or a 0. This type of computing is referred to as binary. A computer's transistors are arranged in grouped arrays called bits. Computers manipulate the 1s and 0s in these bits to calculate and process data.

Quantum computers also have bits. They are referred to as qubits. Instead of being made up of transistors, a qubit is made up of subatomic particles. Unlike a transistor that can only have two states, 1 or 0, these qubits can have an additional quantum state: 1, 0, and both 1 and 0 all at the same time. This is the part where I usually lose people, so let's use an analogy to continue the idea. In the 1930s, Erwin Schrödinger, an Austrian theoretical physicist, used the analogy of a cat in a box to explain how quantum states work.[96] For all you cat lovers, I want to be clear, this is just a thought experiment to explain how subatomic particles behave. No cats were harmed in the thinking of this experiment.

---

[96] Rouse, M. (2017). "Schrödinger's Cat." TechTarget. Retrieved from http://whatis.techtarget.com/definition/Schrodingers-cat.

The experiment goes like this: You grab a steel box, a cat, and some lethal poison. You put the cat and the poison in the box and close the lid. At this point, the cat is in a binary state: the cat hasn't eaten the poison and is alive, or the cat ate the poison and is dead (1 or 0). Because the box is opaque, you cannot see if the cat is dead or alive. So if you ask someone, "What are the possible states of the cat?" the answer would not be either dead (0) or alive (1), but both answers are currently possible (0 and 1). It is only when you open the box that you discover the state of the cat. In the same way, a qubit is in both states until measured. This means that from a computation point of view you are not restricted to perform a process with only a 1 or 0; you can process both a 1 or 0 individually or both states simultaneously. Still with me?

A qubit can perform multiple computations simultaneously. When looking at a single qubit, three possible answers, instead of two, doesn't seem like a big deal. Remember, though, a processor is comprised of many bits. Bits, with all possible states represented, do not add or multiply in their ability to process— it is a factorial function. This means that quantum computers can tackle problems that would require a conventional computer literally billions of years to solve.

If you take a simple problem of parking fifteen cars in fifteen parking spots and ask a computer to report all of the different combinations of how to park all the cars in all of the spots, a quantum computer could process all of the different combinations at once because it can consider all possibilities at once.

A conventional computer would have to compute every possible variation, one variation at a time. For regular bit processors that are the same speed as a qubit processor, it would take 1,300,000,000,000 (1.3 gazillion) times longer to complete this task. That's just fifteen cars and fifteen parking spots. If you have thirty cars and thirty parking spots, it's not twice the processing time for a conventional computer, it's much more: $2.6 \times 10^{32}$ times longer or 2,600,000,000,000,000,000,000,000,000,000,000 times longer. Conventional computers are really good at quickly solving problems with a specific set of variables but not very useful for complex problems. Quantum computers are really good at solving complex problems with a large number of variables.

Historically, there are many problems that computers have not been able to solve relating to big data that are now in reach due to the possible applications of quantum computers: complex modeling of weather patterns; simulating the folding of proteins for the purpose of designing powerful new drugs; simulation of financial markets to more accurately predict outcomes; molecular simulation in the fields of chemistry and materials science, just to name a few. The two applications that relate to the Internet are targeted marketing and the holy grail of quantum computing: artificial intelligence.

## GETTING TO KNOW YOU EVEN MORE!

Looking at the amount of data Google collects on its users for the purpose of marketing through its myriad "free" applications, it's no surprise that they were one of the first companies to adopt quantum computing. Google has been utilizing quantum computing technology since 2013.[97] It is one of the largest technology companies with their hands in many sectors: search, cloud computing, hardware, autonomous vehicles, and more. It's hard to say exactly how they are using this new processing power,

---

[97] Wikimedia Foundation, Inc. (2017). List of companies involved in quantum computing or communication. Retrieved from https://en.wikipedia.org/wiki/List_of_companies_involved_in_quantum_computing_or_communication.

but it's a safe bet that they have, on some scale, tested quantum computing on analyzing their users' data.

As we discussed in chapter 2, Internet companies like Google and Facebook are moving from simple targeted marketing—presenting marketing that is tailored to your specific interests—to social engineering, attempting to predict your online behavior. Predicting human behavior requires calculating an enormous set of variables. Quantum cognition is a new theory that suggests the mathematical principles behind quantum computing could be used to better understand another notoriously inexplicable area of study: human behavior.[98]

Understanding how well Internet companies like Facebook have been able to utilize conventional computers to influence human behavior through social engineering on an extremely basic level, we as Internet users should be keenly aware that with the development of quantum computers we have only seen the tip of the iceberg.

Quantum computers are still very much in their infancy. The first production quantum computer was released by D-Wave in 2007.[99] It's difficult to say exactly how effective these machines will be at predicting and influencing human behavior. What is clear is how quickly the technology is developing. Since 1999, D-Wave (the leading quantum computing company), in a relatively short amount of time, went from a small start-up to building quantum computers for world-class organizations and institutions: Lockheed Martin, Google, NASA, USC, USRA,

---

[98] Beck, J. (2015). "How 'Quantum Cognition' Can Explain Humans' Irrational Behaviors." Retrieved from https://www.theatlantic.com/health/archive/2015/09/how-quantum-cognition-can-explain-humans-irrational-behaviors/405787/.

[99] "D-Wave: The Quantum Computing Company." Retrieved from https://www.dwavesys.com/our-company/meet-d-wave.

and Los Alamos National Laboratory. Additionally, D-Wave has been granted more than 140 U.S. patents.

## JUST WHAT DO YOU THINK YOU ARE DOING, DAVE? _

Although computers are very good at calculations and running programs, anyone who has used a computer for any length of time will recognize that they are not the most intelligent devices. They rely entirely on programs to know what to do at any given time.

Additionally, conventional computers that you and I use every day are limited to algorithms that must be processed through yes/no binary logic. Computers are not so good at problem-solving when answers are "maybe" or "kind of." Answers such as "maybe" or "kind of" are easy for humans to answer. To be fair, we humans have a bit of an advantage over our binary friends. God's design of our processor (our brain) in comparison to even the most advanced computer is still a ridiculous comparison. Our brain's ability to quickly analyze and make decisions to an infinite number of problems is astounding.

While quantum computing is nowhere near eclipsing our brain's capacity for analyzing and reasoning complex problems, it is a huge leap forward from the binary processing of our current technology and a giant leap forward in computers understanding and emulating human behavior.

In 2014, a huge milestone in the development of artificial intelligence was achieved when the Turing Test was passed.[100] This test measures a machine's ability to exhibit intelligent behavior

---

100   BC News (2014). "Computer AI passes Turing test in 'world first.'" June 9. Retrieved from http://www.bbc.com/news/technology-27762088.

equivalent to, or indistinguishable from, human behavior. The Turing Test was developed by Alan Turing. He proposed that a human evaluator would judge natural language conversations between a human and a machine designed to generate human-like responses. The evaluator was aware that one of the two parties in conversation was a machine; all participants were separated from one another. The conversation was limited to a text-only channel, such as a computer keyboard and screen, so that the result would not depend on the machine's ability to render words as speech. If the evaluator cannot reliably tell the machine from the human, the machine is said to have passed the test.

## WILL THE REAL REALITY PLEASE STAND UP? _

If you happen to be a supermodel, you would know the date February 19, 1990. It was a pretty significant date. This was the date that the first version of the application Photoshop was released.[101] At the time, it wasn't much more impressive than Microsoft Paint. Since its inception, it has become a staple of the photography industry, so much so that Photoshop is not only a noun, but a verb. According to Merriam-Webster: to alter (a digital image) with Photoshop software or other image-editing software especially in a way that distorts reality (as for deliberately deceptive purposes).[102]

If you have ever stood in a supermarket checkout line and thought to yourself, *Gosh! Those models on magazine covers look*

---

[101] Hohweiler, J. 2016). "History of Photoshop." August 22. Retrieved from https://www.greaterthangatsby.com/history-of-photoshop/.

[102] Merriam-Webster, Incorporated (2017). Retrieved from https://www.merriam-webster.com/dictionary/photoshop.

*amazing. I could never look that good.* The truth is, those models could never look that good either. Thanks to Photoshop, no one in print is actually who they are in reality. These images are digitally perfected versions of people. Thanks to programs like After Effects, the same is true with movies.[103] In the last 25 years, computers have made fantasy a reality in print and film.

What if they could do that in real life? That's basically the idea behind Augmented Reality (AR): an enhanced version of reality created by the use of technology to overlay digital information.[104] The most common version of this technology are the AR apps for your smartphone. In the summer of 2016, Pokémon GO took the app stores by storm with 65 million active users every month.[105] If you're not familiar with the app, during the summers of 2016 and 2017, it was the reason all the kids and nerds of all ages in your neighborhood were standing on street corners aimlessly staring at their phones. In the game, players must search for virtual creatures that appear projected onto their real surroundings on the screen of their phone. In September of 2016, there were an estimated total of 113,993 incidents reported, where drivers and pedestrians had been distracted by the game.[106]

---

[103] Scott, S. (2016). "See what's possible with After Effects." Retrieved from https://helpx.adobe.com/after-effects/how-to/what-is-after-effects-cc.html.

[104] Reality Technologies (2016). "Augmented Reality." Retrieved from http://www.realitytechnologies.com/augmented-reality.

[105] Anthony, S. (2017). "A year in, millions still play Pokémon Go (and will likely attend its festival)." Retrieved from https://arstechnica.com/gaming/2017/07/a-year-in-millions-still-play-pokemon-go-and-will-likely-attend-its-festival/.

[106] Borland, S. (2016). Don't Pokémon Go and drive! More than 110,000 road accidents in the US were caused by the game in just 10 days. Retrieved from http://www.dailymail.co.uk/sciencetech/article-3793050/Don-t-Pokemon-drive-110-000-road-accidents-caused-game-just-10-days.html.

Pokémon GO is just one of many apps in this new digital AR arena. Almost every app developer is evaluating how to leverage this technology to enhance their product offerings. Furniture giant IKEA has added AR to their Amikasa - 3D Floor Planner. The app allows you to utilize the camera on your phone to test how their furniture pieces will look in your house. Simply point your phone at the empty corner of the room where you need to add that comfy oversized recliner. Not only will the app project the 3D image of the chair in your living room, to scale, but as you move around the space, the app will accurately display the furniture from all angles as if it was actually there.

As you can imagine, producers of pornography apps and content are paying close attention to this technology. It is the obvious next step in the evolution of pornography. As pornography has quickly moved into virtually reality (VR) with the development of platforms like Google's Daydream (formally Cardboard) and GoPro's Jump 360 VR, AR is likely the next step. If you would like to learn more about current VR tech from Google and GoPro, I would recommend watching Google Data Center 360° Tour on YouTube.

## DID I SAY THAT? _

AR is not just involved in what you can see. Adobe (the makers of Photoshop) recently released an audio editing and generating prototype software called VoCo that enables novel editing and generation of audio.[107] It has been popularly dubbed "the Photoshop of voice." Voice editing is nothing new. Ever since

[107] Carmichael, J. (2016). "Adobe's 'VoCo' Can Put Words in Your Mouth." Retrieved from https://www.inverse.com/article/23350-adobe-voco.

Edison created the phonograph, the potential for editing what someone says and changing it to something else has existed. Sometimes this is for the sake of cleaning up a recorded interview or speech; removing the "likes," "ums," and "uhs" we all say when we are speaking publicly. Sometimes soundbites are cut to promote a news story. There have also been cases where someone nefariously rearranges the words spoken in a speech for the sake of communicating something that the speaker never intended to say.

VoCo takes these scenarios a step further. With just 20 minutes of a speaker's speech—for VoCo to learn their speech patterns— VoCo can generate audio of the speaker saying anything you tell VoCo you want them to say, including words that were not in their 20-minute speech.

## LOOK WHO'S TALKING!

A new video technology that goes hand-in-hand with VoCo is an application called Face2Face.[108] It is a real-time capture and reenactment software. Although the current version is in a beta-testing stage, the tests are pretty impressive. The software, like VoCo, takes samples of people in videos, modeling their face in a digital environment. Then the user can model their own face. Once mapped, using a web camera, the user can talk and make facial gestures; meanwhile, in real time, the program will take the pre-recorded video and make the subject match the user's facial features.

With the combination of these two applications and a video of someone speaking, you could create a new video in which the

---

[108] Hart, M. (2016). "'Face2Face' Tech Allows for Total Manipulation of Any Face." Retrieved from https://nerdist.com/face2face-tech-allows-for-total-manipulation-of-any-face/.

subject can say whatever you want them to say. If you would like to see examples of these technologies, search on YouTube for "VoCo test" and "Face2Face capture."

In this chapter, I have described a ton of technology that may leave your head spinning. I have also refrained from drawing conclusions as I have described what is headed our way. This was intentional. Given how much of an Internet expert you have become from reading this book, I trust that as you have read this chapter, your brain is already starting to connect the dots. The truth is that these are just predictions of what is likely to happen. In the next five to ten years, there is a good chance the most influential developments of the Internet don't even exist yet. To reiterate my statement from the beginning of this chapter, hopefully you have had an opportunity to ponder future implications of new tech. I believe the exercise of thinking how upcoming changes to the Internet affect us and those who we influence is likely more important than the information itself.

Now that you have had some time to absorb the future, I would like to share my thoughts on what it all means. There are some key elements we can piece together to reveal the puzzling image of our future. The era of quantum computing offers the ability of Internet companies to create an artificial intelligence that will not only be indistinguishable from a real human, but capable of predicting our behaviors. Through the process of augmented reality, our digital world will begin to reach past the screen into our physical world, taking on the likeness of any digitized person. Living in online fantasy could eventually amount to your closest relationships not consisting of real people but merely of projected polished computer simulations designed to increase consumerism.

Regardless of the accuracy to which I have predicted the next big thing for the Internet, one thing I'm quite certain of:

THE INTERNET OF THE FUTURE WILL BECOME INCREASINGLY
MORE DIFFICULT TO KNOW WHAT IS REAL AND WHAT IS
NOT; TO KNOW WHO IS REAL AND WHO IS NOT.

## THE RED PILL IS A CHOICE _

Looking at what the future of technology holds and the seemingly inevitable direction of our society, moving further and further from reality, it would be remiss to overlook the glaringly obvious resemblance to *The Matrix* analogy from chapter 0 of this book. The epic force of targeted marketing has forged the symbolic alliance of man and machine. The computers have permeated every aspect of our lives with false reality—for our brain to easily escape from reality—in exchange for the powerful advertising dollar justifying the machines' existence. In writing this chapter I'm reminded of the red pill-blue pill scene from the movie, *The Matrix*:

*Morpheus: Unfortunately, no one can be...told what the Matrix is. You have to see it for yourself. [Opens pillbox, empties contents into his palms, outstretched his hands]. This is your last chance. After this, there is no turning back. You take the blue pill [opens his right hand revealing blue pill], the story ends. You wake up in your bed and believe whatever you want to believe. You take the red pill [opens his left hand revealing red pill], you stay in Wonderland, and I show you how deep the rabbit hole goes. [Neo, after a pause, reaches for the red pill]. Morpheus: Remember, all I'm offering is the truth. Nothing more.*[109]

---

109  Wachowski, L. & Wachowski, L. (1999). *The Matrix*. Silver Pictures.

My hope is that, in the process of reading this book, you have received truth and gained a new perspective of the Internet: how most of us use it and how it uses us. The most notable difference between the movie and our world is that unlike Neo, our choice is not a one-time, all-or-nothing experience; rather, we need the daily *red pill* dose of reality.

Embracing reality is a choice that we can quickly forget or overlook. We are always just a few keystrokes or clicks away from fantasy—believing that how we engage online has no effect on our real relationships. The *blue pill* in our world is not so much a choice as it is an awareness. Anyone can move through the world and "believe whatever they want to believe." We must wrestle with the barrage of false messages our digital world proposes:

*Your value is directly proportional to the number of followers, likes, and posts to your social network. Shallow meme-emoji 160-character communication is a real and empathetic form of communication. It is easier to be vulnerable online than with real people and real relationships. A polished-edited-Photoshop version life online is more beautiful than imperfect reality.*

I think this is both a good and a bad thing. It would be great to trust our gut, take the plunge, and unplug—never to return to the illusion of false reality again. To once and for all move from the cocoon of a blind participant in the system of false reality to a reckless vigilante of freedom. This, however, is not the world in which we live. Jesus declares our place in the world of false reality.

*My prayer is not that you take them out of the world but that you protect them from the evil one. They are not of the world, even as I am not of it.*
JOHN 17:15-16

### 8

## CHAPTER RECAP
## HIGHLIGHTS FROM "WHAT THE FUTURE HOLDS"

**Predicting the Future.** As stated, our goal is to answer the question: *How can we positively influence the next generation?* With that purpose in mind, I felt it necessary to not only explore the current reality of the Internet today, but additionally, to do my best to identify what the future of the Internet holds.

**Internet Access.** Internet access is expected to exceed 80 percent of the world's population by the year 2030. By the year 2020 it is estimated that the Internet will have 10 times the amount of data.

**Technological Convergence.** Technological convergence—the concept that every device is connected to the Internet and will uniquely communicate information to the user—will also continue to accelerate in growth. In the very near future, just about every device that uses electricity will be online.

**Quantum Computing.** Quantum computers can tackle problems that would require a conventional computer literally billions of years to solve. Historically, there are many problems that computers have not been able to solve relating to big data that are now in reach due to the possible applications of quantum computers.

**Predicting Human Behavior.** Internet companies like Google and Facebook are moving from simple targeted marketing—presenting marketing that is tailored to your specific interests—to social engineering, attempting to predict your online behavior.

**The Human Brain.** God's design of our processor (our brain) in comparison to even the most advanced computer is still a ridiculous comparison. Our brain's ability to quickly analyze and make decisions to an infinite number of problems is astounding.

**Augmented Reality.** Augmented Reality (AR) is an enhanced version of reality created by the use of technology to overlay digital information. The most common version of this technology are the AR apps for your smartphone.

**Look who's Talking!** With the combination of apps like VoCo and Face2Face, you could create a video in which the subject says whatever you want them to say.

**What We Know?** In the next five to ten years, there is a good chance that the most influential developments of the Internet don't even exist yet.

**What does this mean?** The era of quantum computing offers the ability of Internet companies to create an artificial intelligence that will not only be indistinguishable from a real human, but also capable of predicting our behaviors.

**Choosing the Red Pill.** Our choice is not a one-time, all-or-nothing experience; rather, we have a need for the daily *red pill* dose of reality. Embracing reality is a choice that we can quickly forget or overlook. We are always just a few keystrokes or clicks away from fantasy, believing that how we engage online has no effect on our real relationships.

# APPENDIX

## GLOSSARY _

**Accountability app**
An accountability app is a software application that records and reports to a predetermined group of users the online activity of each user.

**Blacklist**
A list of Internet web addresses for which a filter automatically denies or blocks access.

**Content filtering** (also known as information filtering)
Content filtering is the use of a program to screen and exclude from access or availability web pages or emails that are deemed objectionable.[110] Content filtering is used by corporations as part of Internet firewall computers and also by home computer owners, especially by parents to screen the content their children have access to from a computer.

**DNS** (**D**omain **N**ame **S**ystem)
The Internet's system for converting alphabetic names into numeric IP addresses.[111] For example, when a web address (URL) is typed into a browser, DNS servers return the IP address

---

[110] TechTarget (2017). "Search Web gateways, from evaluation to sealed deal." Retrieved from http://searchsecurity.techtarget.com/definition/content-filtering.

[111] PCMag Digital Group (2017). Encyclopedia. Retrieved from https://www.pcmag.com/encyclopedia/term/41620/dns.

of the web server associated with that name. In this made-up example, the DNS converts the URL www.company.com into the IP address 204.0.8.51. Without DNS, you would have to type the series of four numbers and dots into your browser to retrieve the website, which you actually can do.

## GPS (Global Positioning System)

A global system of U.S. navigational satellites developed to provide precise positional and velocity data and global time synchronization for air, sea, and land travel. An electronic system that uses these satellites to determine the position of a vehicle, person, or locations.

## Hardware

Physical internal and external parts of a computer and related devices.[112] Internal hardware devices include motherboards, hard drives, and RAM. External hardware includes devices such as monitors, keyboards, and printers.

## IP Address (Internet Protocol)

The IP Address is a unique address that a device such as a personal computer, tablet, or smartphone uses to identify itself and communicate with other devices in the IP network.[113] Any device connected to the IP network must have a unique IP Address within the network. An IP address is analogous to a street address or telephone number in that it is used to uniquely identify an entity.

---

[112] TechTerms (2017). Hardware Definition. Retrieved from https://techterms.com/definition/hardware.

[113] IP Location (2017). "What is an IP Address?" Retrieved from https://www.iplocation.net/ip-address.

**ISP** (**I**nternet **S**ervice **P**rovider)
ISP refers to a company that provides Internet services, including personal and business access to the Internet.[114] For a monthly fee, the service provider delivers a software package, equipped with a modem, so you can access the Internet.

**LAN** (**L**ocal **A**rea **N**etwork)
A LAN is a network that connects computers and other devices in a relatively small area, typically a single building or a group of buildings.

**Modem**
A hardware device that connects a computer or LAN to the Internet. The word modem is short for modulator/demodulator, referring to the first generation of modems that converted digital signals from a computer to analog audio signals that were transmitted over telephone lines. Modern modems, like cable modems or fiber optic modems, are a bit of a misnomer. They do not convert digital signals to analog (modulate/demodulate signals); rather, they convert digital network signals to digital cable signals, or fiber optic (pulsed light) digital signals. The conversion is not digital to analog but short distance transmission technology (ethernet) to long distance transmission (fiber, cable, etc.).

**Proxy**
A Proxy is another computer in the Internet that serves as a hub through which requests are processed. The proxy allows a user to request sites the proxy displays for the user without filtering or reporting to a user's accountability app.

---

[114] ITBusinessEdge (2017). "IPS – Internet service provider." Retrieved from http://www.webopedia.com/TERM/I/ISP.html.

**Router**

A router is a hardware device that forwards data between a LAN and the Internet. Most newer routers incorporate WiFi.

**URL** (**U**niform **R**esource **L**ocator)

A URL is the web address to a specific website on the Internet; e.g., puredesire.org.

**Whitelist**

A list of Internet web address to which a filter automatically allows access.

**WiFi**

A technology that allows personal computers, tablets, and smartphones to communicate wirelessly via radio signal.

# INTERNET ADDICTION TEST _

Internet Addiction Test (IAT) is a reliable and valid measure of addictive use of the Internet, developed by Dr. Kimberly Young.[115] It consists of 20 questions that measure mild, moderate, and severe levels of Internet addiction. For best scoring results, please answer each of the following questions.

1. How often do you find that you stay online longer than you intended?

   ☐ Rarely  ☐ Occasionally  ☐ Frequently  ☐ Often  ☐ Always  ☐ N/A

2. How often do you neglect household chores to spend more time online?

   ☐ Rarely  ☐ Occasionally  ☐ Frequently  ☐ Often  ☐ Always  ☐ N/A

3. How often do you prefer the excitement of the Internet to intimacy with your partner?

   ☐ Rarely  ☐ Occasionally  ☐ Frequently  ☐ Often  ☐ Always  ☐ N/A

4. How often do you form new relationships with fellow online users?

   ☐ Rarely  ☐ Occasionally  ☐ Frequently  ☐ Often  ☐ Always  ☐ N/A

5. How often do others in your life complain to you about the amount of time you spend online?

   ☐ Rarely  ☐ Occasionally  ☐ Frequently  ☐ Often  ☐ Always  ☐ N/A

6. How often do your grades or school work suffer because of the amount of time you spend online?

   ☐ Rarely  ☐ Occasionally  ☐ Frequently  ☐ Often  ☐ Always  ☐ N/A

[115] Young, K. (1998). *Caught in the Net: How to Recognize the Signs of Internet Addiction— and a Winning Strategy for Recovery*. New York, NY: John Wiley & Sons, Inc.

**7.** How often do you check your email before something else that you need to do?

☐ Rarely  ☐ Occasionally  ☐ Frequently  ☐ Often  ☐ Always  ☐ N/A

**8.** How often does your job performance or productivity suffer because of the Internet?

☐ Rarely  ☐ Occasionally  ☐ Frequently  ☐ Often  ☐ Always  ☐ N/A

**9.** How often do you become defensive or secretive when anyone asks you what you do online?

☐ Rarely  ☐ Occasionally  ☐ Frequently  ☐ Often  ☐ Always  ☐ N/A

**10.** How often do you block out disturbing thoughts about your life with soothing thoughts of the Internet?

☐ Rarely  ☐ Occasionally  ☐ Frequently  ☐ Often  ☐ Always  ☐ N/A

**11.** How often do you find yourself anticipating when you will go online again?

☐ Rarely  ☐ Occasionally  ☐ Frequently  ☐ Often  ☐ Always  ☐ N/A

**12.** How often do you fear that life without the Internet would be boring, empty, and joyless?

☐ Rarely  ☐ Occasionally  ☐ Frequently  ☐ Often  ☐ Always  ☐ N/A

**13.** How often do you snap, yell, or act annoyed if someone bothers you while you are online?

☐ Rarely  ☐ Occasionally  ☐ Frequently  ☐ Often  ☐ Always  ☐ N/A

**14.** How often do you lose sleep due to late night log-ins?

☐ Rarely  ☐ Occasionally  ☐ Frequently  ☐ Often  ☐ Always  ☐ N/A

**15.** How often do you feel preoccupied with the Internet when offline, or fantasize about being online?

☐ Rarely  ☐ Occasionally  ☐ Frequently  ☐ Often  ☐ Always  ☐ N/A

**16.** How often do you find yourself saying, "Just a few more minutes" when online?

☐ Rarely ☐ Occasionally ☐ Frequently ☐ Often ☐ Always ☐ N/A

**17.** How often do you try to cut down the amount of time you spend online and fail?

☐ Rarely ☐ Occasionally ☐ Frequently ☐ Often ☐ Always ☐ N/A

**18.** How often do you try to hide how long you've been online?

☐ Rarely ☐ Occasionally ☐ Frequently ☐ Often ☐ Always ☐ N/A

**19.** How often do you choose to spend more time online over going out with others?

☐ Rarely ☐ Occasionally ☐ Frequently ☐ Often ☐ Always ☐ N/A

**20.** How often do you feel depressed, moody, or nervous when you are offline, which goes away once you are back online?

☐ Rarely ☐ Occasionally ☐ Frequently ☐ Often ☐ Always ☐ N/A

When finished, total the scores for each question using the following scale:

| N/A | 0 points | x | = |
|------|----------|---|---|
| Rarely | 1 point | x | = |
| Occasionally | 2 points | x | = |
| Frequently | 3 points | x | = |
| Often | 4 points | x | = |
| Always | 5 points | x | = |
| **Total** | | | = |

The higher your score (total points), the greater level of addiction.

**20 – 49 points:** You are an average online user. You may surf the web a bit too long at times, but you have control over your usage.

**50 – 79 points:** You are experiencing occasional or frequent problems because of the Internet. You should consider its full impact on your life.

**80 – 100 points:** Your Internet use is causing significant problems in your life. You should elevate the impact of the Internet on your life and address the problems directly caused by your Internet use.

If you are experiencing occasional, frequent, or significant problems because of your Internet use, and want to talk with a Sexual Addiction Professional, contact Pure Desire Ministries:

- 503.489.0237
- info@puredesire.org
- puredesire.org/counseling

# INTERNET USE PLAN _

An Internet Use Plan empowers you to use technology in a way that reinforces healthy behaviors. Take some the time to sit down and look honestly at the way you use technology before completing the Internet Use Plan. It will be to your advantage if you are honest and specific in your plan. You should reassess your Internet Use Plan once every three months, whenever you add a new device or app to your life, or when you join a new social network.

Technology itself is not evil. The goal is for your use of technology to support your healthy behaviors rather than being a downfall. While a website or app might not specifically encourage negative behaviors, pay attention to how you might be using them to isolate.

If you have a spouse or family, consider creating an Internet Use Plan together. As you create a plan as a family, ask yourself, "Does this match our family values?" A family plan creates a culture of health, openness, and accountability for you and your children.

**Name:** _____

**What devices do you use?**

*Examples: Work cellphone, personal laptop, family computer, game console, etc.*

## Where is it okay to use those devices?

*Examples: Living room, coffee shop, etc.*

Device: _____ Location(s): _____

Device: _____ Location(s): _____

Device: _____ Location(s): _____

Device: _____ Location(s): _____

Device: _____ Location(s): _____

## Where is it not okay to use those devices?

*Examples: Bedroom, bathroom, etc.*

Device: _____ Location(s): _____

Device: _____ Location(s): _____

Device: _____ Location(s): _____

Device: _____ Location(s): _____

Device: _____ Location(s): _____

## What websites/apps have been detrimental to your health?

Include any websites and apps that have been a problem for you,
even if you haven't visited them for a while. Remove or block
these from your devices if they are currently accessible to you.
*Examples: YouTube, Facebook, etc.*

_____

_____

_____

_____

_____

_____

**What websites and apps have supported your health?**
Include websites and apps that help you maintain structure, accountability, and community.
*Examples: Pure Desire Ministries, rTribe, etc.*

---

### ❯ SAFETY SOFTWARE

**What filters are you using?**
*Examples: No explicit lyrics in music apps, Google SafeSearch, OpenDNS, YouTube Restricted Mode, having a password for making changes to your device that only your accountability partner has access to, etc.*

---

**What accountability apps are you using?**
Your accountability app should work on your device(s) and provide understandable reports to your accountability partners.
*Examples: Accountable2you, Covenant Eyes, etc.*

## Who are your accountability partners?

You should have at least two accountability partners, people who will follow up with you about your accountability reports. Group members make great accountability partners. Your spouse does not.

## What loopholes are you aware of?

It is possible to get around any filtering or accountability app.
*Example: My game console is not compatible with accountability software.*

## What actions can you take to close the loopholes?

*Example: Our family has a rule that no one is allowed to use the Xbox without someone else in the room.*

# FAMILY VALUES EXERCISE _

This Family Values Exercise emphasizes relationship rather than rules. Rebellious behaviors subside in teens when family members individually create a word and picture collage of what they would like their family to look like, then share their collages. A family of four with two teen girls started with collages and then came up the example of family values presented here. This amazing tool helped this family make some drastic changes. When teens have input into family decisions, they gain ownership. When healthy values are internalized, kids will take those values with them when they leave home.

## ❯ SAMPLE FAMILY VALUES

- Unconditional love
- Loving God
- Integrity
- Internal beauty
- Happiness
- Peace

- Respect
- Express feelings
- Communication
- Self-care
- Responsibility
- Having fun

## ❯ SAMPLE FAMILY VALUES BEHAVIORS

- Communicating respectfully
- Finishing chores
- Completing homework on time
- Spending time in the Word
- Picking up the trash
- Cleaning up their mess
- Cleaning up their dirty dishes
- Going to bed on time

- Eating meals with the family
- Taking shoes off in the house
- Feeding pets
- Taking the dog for a walk
- Brushing their teeth
- Coming home before curfew
- Making dinner
- Keeping grades up
- Mowing the lawn
- Having devotional time
- Helping a sibling
- Following through on promises
- Being on time
- Responding to negative emotions in a healthy way
- Accepting consequences
- Being present with family
- Respecting others' personal space
- Being open and honest

## ⊙ SAMPLE REWARDS

**Trust/Rewards Level 1**

- Dinner out
- Roller-blading
- Bike-riding
- Hiking
- Summer activities
- Winter activities
- Babysitting
- Trampoline
- Hot tub
- Fire pit
- Roasting marshmallows

## Trust/Rewards Level 2

- Frozen yogurt
- Late bedtime
- Playdates
- Boat w/ family
- Summer activities w/ friends
- Winter activities w/ friends
- TV/Wii
- Movies
- Go to neighbor's house
- Practice driving
- Camping w/ family

## Trust/Rewards Level 3

- Skating rink (supervised)
- Home alone
- Overnight sleepover
- Boat w/ friends
- Pool w/ friends
- Mall w/ friends
- Phone (w/o camera)
- Camping w/ friends

## Trust/Rewards Level 4

- Skating rink (unsupervised)
- Movie w/ friends
- Weekend sleepover
- Supervised group activities
- Phone (w/ camera)
- Computer
- Water park

## Trust/Rewards Level 5

- Go on family vacation
- Go on vacation w/ a friend
- Driving
- Unsupervised group activities
- Dating at 16 years old

## ❯ SAMPLE BEHAVIOR AGAINST FAMILY VALUES

### Severity Level 1

- Continued arguing
- Continued bickering
- Continued sarcasm
- Continued annoyance
- Not finishing chores
- Homework late (2 days)
- Not picking up trash (>1 hr)
- Not cleaning up mess (>1 hr)
- Leaving dirty dishes (>1 hr)
- Not going to bed on time
- Not eating/missing meals
- Name-calling
- Shoes in house after warning
- Dog upstairs
- Not brushing teeth
- Past curfew (15 mins)

### Severity Level 2

- Yelling
- Profanity
- Severe sarcasm
- Severe annoyance
- Not doing chores
- Not picking up trash (>24 hrs)
- Listening to inappropriate music
- Homework late (1 week)
- Not cleaning up (>24 hrs)
- Leaving dirty dishes (>24 hrs)
- Minimal physical fighting
- Gossip
- Past curfew (30 mins)

### Severity Level 3

- Uncontrolled rage
- Lying
- Deceiving
- Cutting class
- Homework late (2 weeks)
- Sneaking
- Not using a bike helmet
- Moderate physical fighting
- Past curfew (1 hr)

## Severity Level 4

- Destroying property (minimal)
- Go to friend's house w/o permission
- Acting inappropriate w/ opposite gender
- Cutting school
- Homework late (1 month)
- Dating/going out before 16 years old
- Inappropriate use of computer
- Severe physical fighting

## Severity Level 5

- Destroying property (severe)
- Completely disobeying family values
- Sexting
- Unsupervised friends of opposite gender at house
- Smoking
- Alcohol
- Drugs
- Grade <C
- Looking at pornography
- Having sex
- Having oral sex
- Heavy petting
- Having unapproved party at the house
- Going to unapproved party
- Going over to friend of opposite gender's house

## ◉ SAMPLE NATURAL CONSEQUENCES

If behavior continues, then the result will be SEPARATION from the family for a specified time.

### Severity Level 1

- No TV (24 hrs)
- No Wii (24 hrs)
- Room time/time-out
- No computer (24 hrs)
- No movies (24 hrs)
- Early bedtime

### Severity Level 2

- No TV (72 hrs)
- No Wii (72 hrs)
- No phone (24 hrs)
- No computer (72 hrs)
- No movies (72 hrs)
- No scheduling playdates
- No boat activities (24 hrs)
- No winter activities (24 hrs)
- No summer activities (24 hrs)

### Severity Level 3

- No TV (1 week)
- No Wii (1 week)
- No phone (3 days)
- No computer (1 week)
- No movies (1 week)
- No skating rink (1 month)
- No sleepovers (1 month)
- No playdates (1 month)
- Apology letter
- No boat activities (1 week)
- No winter activities (1 week)
- No summer activities (1 week)

### Severity Level 4

- No TV (2 weeks)
- No Wii (2 weeks)
- No phone (1 month)
- No movies (1 month)
- No skating rink (3 months)
- No sleepovers (3 months)
- No playdates (3 months)
- Limited home activity
- No boat activities (1 month)
- No winter activities (1 month)
- No summer activities (1 month)

**Severity Level 5**
*(Time to be Determined)*

- No phone
- No computer
- No movies
- No skating rink
- No sleepovers
- No playdates

- No being home alone
- No boat activity
- No winter activity
- No summer activity
- Counseling
- Community service

## ❯ CREATING YOUR OWN FAMILY VALUES

Ask each family member to create a word and/or picture collage about what they want their family to look like. Then brainstorm a list of possible family values. Make your own list, based on what individuals in your family think are important based on your family collages. Discuss the list and allow each family member to "vote" for 5 to 10 values represented by the family collages, those they (as a family) want to commit to doing. (Vote using sticky dots or simply putting a check mark by their choices.) After the "voting," decide which values on the list most family members want to adopt.

Next, list behaviors that go against family values. Decide what goes on the natural consequences chart and then create a rewards chart. Have a family member design your charts, ensuring that all family members understand how your Family Values System will work. Post the charts for all to see, as a reminder of your commitment to building shared values.

# EMPATHY QUOTIENT _

The Empathy Quotient (EQ) is a 60-item questionnaire designed to measure empathy in adults. The test was developed by Simon Baron-Cohen at ARC (the Autism Research Centre) at the University of Cambridge.[116],[117],[118]

Clinically, the empathy measurements provided by the EQ are used by mental health professionals in assessing the level of social impairment in certain disorders like autism. However, since levels of empathy vary significantly between individuals, even between those without any mental health disorders, it is also suitable for use as a casual measure of temperamental empathy by and for the general population.

Below is a list of statements. Please read each statement carefully and rate how strongly you agree or disagree with it by checking the box next to your answer. There are no right or wrong answers, or trick questions.

**1.** I can easily tell if someone else wants to enter a conversation.

☐ Strongly Agree ☐ Slightly Agree ☐ Slightly Disagree ☐ Strongly Disagree

**2.** I prefer animals to humans.

☐ Strongly Agree ☐ Slightly Agree ☐ Slightly Disagree ☐ Strongly Disagree

**3.** I try to keep up with the current trends and fashions.

☐ Strongly Agree ☐ Slightly Agree ☐ Slightly Disagree ☐ Strongly Disagree

[116] S Baron-Cohen, S Wheelwright. *The Empathy Quotient: An Investigation Of Adults With Asperger Syndrome Or High Functioning Autism, And Normal Sex Differences*. 34(2): J Autism Dev Disord 163-75. 2004.

[117] VL Ruggieri. *[Empathy, Social Cognition And Autism Spectrum Disorders]*. 56 Suppl 1: Rev Neurol S13-21. 2013.

[118] E Sucksmith, C Allison, S Baron-Cohen, B Chakrabarti, RA Hoekstra. *Empathy And Emotion Recognition In People With Autism, First-degree Relatives, And Controls*. 51(1): Neuropsychologia 98-105. 2013.

**43.** Friends usually talk to me about their problems since they feel I am very understanding.

☐ Strongly Agree ☐ Slightly Agree ☐ Slightly Disagree ☐ Strongly Disagree

**44.** I can sense if I am intruding, even if the other person doesn't tell me.

☐ Strongly Agree ☐ Slightly Agree ☐ Slightly Disagree ☐ Strongly Disagree

**45.** I often start new hobbies but quickly become bored with them and move on to something else.

☐ Strongly Agree ☐ Slightly Agree ☐ Slightly Disagree ☐ Strongly Disagree

**46.** People sometimes tell me that I have gone too far with teasing.

☐ Strongly Agree ☐ Slightly Agree ☐ Slightly Disagree ☐ Strongly Disagree

**47.** I would be too nervous to go on a big roller coaster.

☐ Strongly Agree ☐ Slightly Agree ☐ Slightly Disagree ☐ Strongly Disagree

**48.** Other people often say I am insensitive, though I don't always see why.

☐ Strongly Agree ☐ Slightly Agree ☐ Slightly Disagree ☐ Strongly Disagree

**49.** If I see a stranger in a group, I think it is up to them to make an effort to join in.

☐ Strongly Agree ☐ Slightly Agree ☐ Slightly Disagree ☐ Strongly Disagree

**50.** I usually stay emotionally detached when watching a movie.

☐ Strongly Agree ☐ Slightly Agree ☐ Slightly Disagree ☐ Strongly Disagree

**51.** I like to be very organized in day-to-day life and often make lists of the chores I have to do.

☐ Strongly Agree ☐ Slightly Agree ☐ Slightly Disagree ☐ Strongly Disagree

**52.** I can tune into how someone else feels rapidly and intuitively.

☐ Strongly Agree  ☐ Slightly Agree  ☐ Slightly Disagree  ☐ Strongly Disagree

**53.** I don't like to take risks.

☐ Strongly Agree  ☐ Slightly Agree  ☐ Slightly Disagree  ☐ Strongly Disagree

**54.** I can easily figure out what another person might want to talk about.

☐ Strongly Agree  ☐ Slightly Agree  ☐ Slightly Disagree  ☐ Strongly Disagree

**55.** I can tell if someone is masking their true emotion.

☐ Strongly Agree  ☐ Slightly Agree  ☐ Slightly Disagree  ☐ Strongly Disagree

**56.** Before making a decision, I always weigh the pros and cons.

☐ Strongly Agree  ☐ Slightly Agree  ☐ Slightly Disagree  ☐ Strongly Disagree

**57.** I don't consciously understand the rules of social situations.

☐ Strongly Agree  ☐ Slightly Agree  ☐ Slightly Disagree  ☐ Strongly Disagree

**58.** I am good at predicting what someone will do.

☐ Strongly Agree  ☐ Slightly Agree  ☐ Slightly Disagree  ☐ Strongly Disagree

**59.** I tend to get emotionally involved with a friend's problems.

☐ Strongly Agree  ☐ Slightly Agree  ☐ Slightly Disagree  ☐ Strongly Disagree

**60.** I can usually appreciate the other person's viewpoint, even if I don't agree with it.

☐ Strongly Agree  ☐ Slightly Agree  ☐ Slightly Disagree  ☐ Strongly Disagree

Upon completion, use the Empathy Quotient (EQ) Scoring Form to calculate your score.

## ❯ EMPATHY QUOTIENT (EQ)[119] SCORING FORM

After completing the Empathy Quotient, use this form to determine your score. Responses that score 1 or 2 points are marked. Other responses score 0. Based on your test answers, circle the corresponding number for each question. Enter the total points for each row in the right column. For your total score, sum all items in the right column.

| # | Strongly Agree | Slightly Agree | Slightly Disagree | Strongly Disagree | Row Points |
|---|---|---|---|---|---|
| 1 | 2 | 1 | 0 | 0 | |
| 2 | 0 | 0 | 0 | 0 | 0 |
| 3 | 0 | 0 | 0 | 0 | 0 |
| 4 | 0 | 0 | 1 | 2 | |
| 5 | 0 | 0 | 0 | 0 | 0 |
| 6 | 2 | 1 | 0 | 0 | |
| 7 | 0 | 0 | 0 | 0 | 0 |
| 8 | 0 | 0 | 1 | 2 | |
| 9 | 0 | 0 | 0 | 0 | 0 |
| 10 | 0 | 0 | 1 | 2 | |
| 11 | 0 | 0 | 1 | 2 | |
| 12 | 0 | 0 | 1 | 2 | |
| 13 | 0 | 0 | 0 | 0 | 0 |
| 14 | 0 | 0 | 1 | 2 | |
| **Page Total:** | | | | | |

[119] Baron-Cohen, S. & Wheelwright, S. (2004). "The Empathy Quotient (EQ). An investigation of adults with Asperger Syndrome or High Functioning Autism, and normal sex differences." *Journal of Autism and Developmental Disorders* 34:163–175

| # | Strongly Agree | Slightly Agree | Slightly Disagree | Strongly Disagree | Row Points |
|---|---|---|---|---|---|
| 15 | 0 | 0 | 1 | 2 | |
| 16 | 0 | 0 | 0 | 0 | 0 |
| 17 | 0 | 0 | 0 | 0 | 0 |
| 18 | 0 | 0 | 1 | 2 | |
| 19 | 2 | 1 | 0 | 0 | |
| 20 | 0 | 0 | 0 | 0 | 0 |
| 21 | 0 | 0 | 1 | 2 | |
| 22 | 2 | 1 | 0 | 0 | |
| 23 | 0 | 0 | 0 | 0 | 0 |
| 24 | 0 | 0 | 0 | 0 | 0 |
| 25 | 2 | 1 | 0 | 0 | |
| 26 | 2 | 1 | 0 | 0 | |
| 27 | 0 | 0 | 1 | 2 | |
| 28 | 0 | 0 | 1 | 2 | |
| 29 | 0 | 0 | 1 | 2 | |
| 30 | 0 | 0 | 0 | 0 | 0 |
| 31 | 0 | 0 | 0 | 0 | 0 |
| 32 | 0 | 0 | 1 | 2 | |
| 33 | 0 | 0 | 0 | 0 | 0 |
| 34 | 0 | 0 | 1 | 2 | |
| 35 | 2 | 1 | 0 | 0 | |
| 36 | 2 | 1 | 0 | 0 | |
| 37 | 2 | 1 | 0 | 0 | |
| 38 | 2 | 1 | 0 | 0 | |
| 39 | 0 | 0 | 1 | 2 | |
| Page Total: | | | | | |

| # | Strongly Agree | Slightly Agree | Slightly Disagree | Strongly Disagree | Row Points |
|---|---|---|---|---|---|
| 40 | 0 | 0 | 0 | 0 | 0 |
| 41 | 2 | 1 | 0 | 0 | |
| 42 | 2 | 1 | 0 | 0 | |
| 43 | 2 | 1 | 0 | 0 | |
| 44 | 2 | 1 | 0 | 0 | |
| 45 | 0 | 0 | 0 | 0 | 0 |
| 46 | 0 | 0 | 1 | 2 | |
| 47 | 0 | 0 | 0 | 0 | 0 |
| 48 | 0 | 0 | 1 | 2 | |
| 49 | 0 | 0 | 1 | 2 | |
| 50 | 0 | 0 | 1 | 2 | |
| 51 | 0 | 0 | 0 | 0 | 0 |
| 52 | 2 | 1 | 0 | 0 | |
| 53 | 0 | 0 | 0 | 0 | 0 |
| 54 | 2 | 1 | 0 | 0 | |
| 55 | 2 | 1 | 0 | 0 | |
| 56 | 0 | 0 | 0 | 0 | 0 |
| 57 | 2 | 1 | 0 | 0 | |
| 58 | 2 | 1 | 0 | 0 | |
| 59 | 2 | 1 | 0 | 0 | |
| 60 | 2 | 1 | 0 | 0 | |
| **Total Score:** | | | | | |

*Higher scores indicate a greater level of empathy.*